The Emperor

of Ice Cream:

The True Story of Häagen-Dazs

Rose Vesel Mattus

with Jeanette Friedman

The Wordsmithy
New Milford, New Jersey
2004

The Emperor of Ice Cream:
The True Story of Häagen-Dazs®

Deigned by The Wordsmithy
Text set in Bookman Old Style

Printed in Canada

Published by The Wordsmithy, LLC
P.O. Box 224
New Milford, NJ 07646

ISBN 0-9748857-0-3

In memory of my husband,
Reuben Mattus,
who was truly the emperor of his domain.

Rose and Reuben Mattus:
The Founders and Creators of
Häagen-Dazs Ice Cream.

Contents

Best wishes
and Peace for the New Year

Jean Mathieu

Introduction

Sweet, silky and smooth, by the scoop or spoon and swished around your mouth, that quintessential treat, ice cream, becomes a sensuous experience on a sultry summer day. In the new millennium, only one ice cream has achieved the legendary status that evokes the heights of gustatory pleasure 365 days a year—the legendary luxury desert, Häagen-Dazs® Ice Cream.*

When it was discovered, it made the news. Movie stars adored it. Prime Ministers and potheads craved it. Food critic Gael Green declared her last wish to be a dish of coffee Häagen-Dazs. Rock star Pat Benatar put a clause into all her road contracts—Häagen-Dazs was delivered to her dressing room daily. And that ultimate hippie, Frank Zappa, posed in a Häagen-Dazs T-shirt with farm-fresh eggs cradled in his arms, surrounded by fat dairy cows.

At first, Häagen-Dazs Ice Cream was hardly glamorous. It was born in the cradle of a difficult business, its founding

---

*Häagen-Dazs® is a registered trademark of H.D.I.P., Inc.

the story of two immigrants who came to America and fought tooth and nail to excel and succeed. In the process, Reuben Mattus, known to his friends and family as Rufky, and to others as Ruby, changed an industry. With his wife, Rose Vesel, at his side, together they built an ice cream empire and a product that endures.

The Häagen-Dazs story is also a classic love story and the story of a family business, with all the usual problems and rewards. Rose and Ruby, childhood sweethearts, worked hard and maintained their integrity to make the best ice cream they could. Their unique product and marketing approach took decades to perfect. At the peak of their career, 65 million pints of Häagen-Dazs were being sold each year—enough to stretch from here to the moon. Now owned by an international conglomerate, the pint count can reach into the far stretches of the universe.

Fancy food historians say Alexander the Great ate fruit-flavored snow cones. Legends say that Marco Polo, Catherine de Médici and King Charles I of England all had something to do with ice cream. Dolly Madison was the first to serve the delicacy in the White House. But the truth is that the American ice cream industry was born in Baltimore in the middle of the 19th century and it was pretty much a summer-only business until the early 1950s. That's when appropriate technology became widely available, and in almost every case, ice cream was as cheap as you could make it—cold and sweet. It sold, especially on hot days, because there was nothing else.

Then along came Reuben Mattus, whose drive and commitment to quality did not let him rest. Rose was always at his side, making sure that if he dreamed it, it would become a reality. That dream was Häagen-Dazs, and it has been a reality ever since.

HAPTER One

*—Time has a mysterious kindness, always giving back
something we lost.*

I was born Rose Vesel, the only daughter of Jewish immigrants from Europe. Together with my parents and four brothers, we lived at 429 Sackman Street, on the first floor of a two-family house, in Brownsville, Brooklyn—one of the poorest neighborhoods in New York City.

The best-looking boy in the neighborhood, Reuben Mattus, lived with his mother, Lea, and older sister, Eleanor, across the street at 424 Sackman Street on the second floor of his uncle's house. His other uncle also lived in the neighborhood, both uncles owning ice cream factories—if you could call them that—right around the corner on Blake Avenue, a block surrounded by ice cream factories. Uncle Nathan Lipitz ran the Big Bear Ice Cream Company and was married to Tillie, a big, wonderful woman. His brother, Sam, and his wife, Rose, owned the

3

Yukon Ice Cream factory, right across the street from Big Bear. The Kroll brothers, neighbors of ours who used to be plumbers, had gone into the ice cream business as well, and their factory was also there.

Reuben's mother was a tough woman with a sharp tongue and iron fist. She also knew how to wield a broom as an offensive weapon—Reuben once had to hide under the bed to get away from her. He and I had a lot in common. He had an Aunt Tillie and an Uncle Nathan, and so did I. Even though we had very little, his mother taught him about charity, as did my parents. He was a Zionist; I was a Zionist. Given our environment and economic station, we both knew about hard work.

Reuben was born in Grodno, Belarus in 1912 or 1913— we were never really sure. Looking at a picture of his parents before World War I, you see a very handsome couple. They owned a gourmet shop in Grodno and lived a typical upper middle-class life until the outbreak of World War I. Reuben's father, fearing a cataclysm that would eventually embrace all of Europe, came to America to explore the possibility of immigration for himself and his family. When he returned to Grodno for his wife and children, he was picked up by the military and sent to the front as an infantryman. In 1916 he was mortally wounded in the Battle of Tannenberg.

All over Europe, as people starved and died in pandemics, Lea and Eleanor were not spared. With his father gone and his mother and sister near death with typhus, Reuben found himself, at age 4, scrounging through garbage looking for scraps to eat. In those terrible days he didn't dream that one day he'd become the purveyor of a luxury food item—the man they'd call The Emperor of Ice Cream.

When Lea and Eleanor recovered from their illnesses and the war ended, Lea continued to sell foodstuffs. One day she was escorted out of her shop by gun-toting communists who accused her of being a black marketer, a crime punishable by death. Maintaining her composure, Lea explained that her prices simply reflected the rising

Lea and Nathan Mattes.

Reuben Mattus.

prices she paid for goods, and proved it on paper. In just a few minutes she had talked her way out of a desperate situation. But from that moment on Lea became a rabid anti-communist.

Reuben's Uncle Sam had already immigrated to the United States and lived in Brooklyn, New York. With the war over, he sent for the rest of his family in 1920. Like hundreds of thousands before them, the family came in steerage to America and arrived in 1921. At Ellis Island, when they called the name Lea Mattes, immigration officials beheld a 30-something short-waisted, buxom lady with steel blue eyes in a round face with a small, straight nose. With her were two small children. Somewhere along the immigration line, the Mattes name became Mattus, but Lea kept the original spelling all her life.

The new "Mattus" family members were held on the island for a few days to see if they suffered from infectious diseases. While there, Reuben enjoyed the food on Ellis Island, especially the softness of American white bread. Years later, whenever there was a scent of chocolate in the air, Reuben would fondly reminisce about the hot cocoa and good food they served the new arrivals. He may have been the only immigrant to remember Ellis Island food fondly, but then again it was a gourmet's delight compared to the garbage cans of Grodno.

In addition to her children, Lea also brought a part of her homeland with her. Grodno had been one of the oldest Jewish communities in Europe—a hotbed of Zionism and socialism, among other idealistic movements—and Lea brought these "isms" with her when she came to America. They would become part of her legacy to her children.

Lea had a good heart, in spite of her tough exterior. A *pushke* (a charity box) was a standard item in all the Jewish households in the neighborhood and the Mattus home was no exception. Every Friday night, before she lit the Sabbath candles, Lea put a few pennies in the *pushke* for the poor.

Lea was someone who believed in a Jewish homeland, and so her son grew up to become a militantly proud Jew who put his money where his mouth was (especially during Israel's War of Independence in 1948). Lea taught her kids to be resilient, too. Whenever Reuben or Eleanor complained about their limited circumstances, she would show them that others had even less than they. Her children were taught to develop deep and sincere feelings for the suffering of others, a compassion and generosity that certainly stayed with Reuben throughout his life.

My parents also struggled. I was born Rivka Rochel Vesel in Manchester, England, in 1916. My mother, Lily Grochowsky, was a beautiful, blue-eyed woman who came from an upper middle class family, but was orphaned as a little girl and raised by her aunt, Mrs. Zelda Stone. With 13 sons of her own, Zelda Stone still intended to do the best she could for my mother, and that basically meant finding her a solid, respectable match.

My father, David Vesel, was a romantic, a poet and would-be musician. He was a former yeshiva *bocher*, a yeshiva student, but the siren's call of the secular world had replaced his world of religion. Tillie Vesel, his sister, became friends with my mother and casually made the initial introduction. When that introduction led to a more serious state of affairs, both families deemed the match inappropriate and furiously opposed any union. Zelda Stone wanted better for her beautiful niece, and the Vesel family, from rabbinical stock, felt the Stones were hardly worthy of such a learned boy. It didn't help that one of Zelda's sons was also in love with my mother.

Confronted by the hopelessness of their situation, my parents eloped to Warsaw. Eventually they found themselves in Paris, where my father made a few francs playing the clarinet. Then they somehow managed to make their way to London, where my mother found work making costumes for the London stage. Known as Mme. Percy, she provided some of the needed income that supported the family. Then we moved to Manchester, where she continued to work in the theater.

Lily Grochowsky.

David Vesel.

Zelda Stone.

Baby Rose Vesel.

My mother was an excellent seamstress and a good businesswoman. (Sometimes I think I inherited my sense of fashion and love of business from her.) One day, discovering some embroidered tablecloths in a Manchester shop, she showed one to my father, and convinced him that she could easily reproduce them. She suggested they try their fortunes in Ireland, where table linens were made. Moving the family to Belfast, my parents set up a factory to manufacture embroidered goods.

Our family was generally happy, but there were still hints of tragedy in our lives. I was considered a "ghost child." Before I was born, my parents had had another child, a daughter, who died in infancy when her nanny dropped her. In some way, they considered me her replacement. (All told, my mother gave birth to eight children and five survived into adulthood.)

Fortunately, the family business prospered and we were able to visit relatives in the British Isles somewhat regularly. One of my earliest childhood memories, when I was about 4 years old, is of visiting an aunt in Scotland.

I don't remember a Jewish community in Belfast, but my parents worked to maintain Jewish traditions in our home. Every Friday night my mother lit candles to welcome the Sabbath. When one of the household servants saw my mother lighting candles and saying the traditional prayer, she asked, "Oh, Mrs. Vesel, did somebody die?" Coming from her Christian tradition, the woman was used to seeing candles as part of the death and mourning ritual.

"No, this is our tradition," my mother told the maid. "We light candles for the Sabbath. We are Jewish."

"You're a Jew?" the maid cried. "I thought Jews had horns and tails."

This was Belfast.

After eight years, the tablecloth factory was bombed by the British during the Black and Tan War and, nearly penniless, my parents boarded a boat bound for the United States.

Immigration Document.
Pictured: Rose, Al and Mom.

We arrived at Ellis Island with Polish passports and I remember an official asking my father what impressed him the most about America. He answered, "The Statue of Liberty." It was 1921, the same year Reuben came to America.

My folks had a tough time getting started in the United States. My mother had given birth to another little boy, but he also died. We moved around a bit—to places like Cherry Street on the Lower East Side in Manhattan—until we wound up on Sackman Street in Brooklyn.

In spite of their problems, Mama and Papa enveloped us in love, gave us a tremendous sense of self-confidence and laughed a lot, through good times and bad. When we arrived in East New York, Mama hung a shingle from the window of our apartment that read, "Madame Wesoly, Seamstress." My brothers, like all young boys, were wild and always in the streets. But even in their old age, they would always retain their youthful sense of humor. Me? I was treated like a brilliant princess and was the apple of my father's eye.

Like my family, Reuben's relatives were hardworking, decent folks. But our neighborhood wasn't the best. Murder, Inc. owned a warehouse across the street from us, where they stored bootleg whiskey. Occasionally we even heard gunshots and saw cops around.

In the Roaring Twenties we had our share of would-be intellectuals who would argue, yell, scream and generally make sure they got their points across—whether it was about the communists, the Zionists, the details of a baseball game or God. In the middle of it all was the local synagogue.

Ideals, of course, were all very well and good—and we talked about them all the time—but people still had to make a living. The Mattus family did it by making ice cream in the summer. Uncle Nathan's Big Bear Ice Cream Company could hardly be described as a vast enterprise: he peddled lemon ices from a horse-drawn cart, after he taught his painted-blue horse to understand his

The Vesel family.

commands in Yiddish. Uncle Sam wasn't much better off at his Yukon company. Of course, Reuben went into the business as well, squeezing lemons by hand for the Italian ices.

Cockeyed Uncle Nathan had a wonderful wife, but his business sense was never too developed. Maybe he was too busy carrying on with the girls in the factory to keep his mind on the store. His son, Eddie, who later became Reuben's brother-in-law, really ran Big Bear. Yes, that's right. Reuben's sister, Eleanor, married her first cousin. To this day I don't know the dynamics of that relationship, but suffice it to say, Eleanor's life with Eddie was never a great one.

To improve his business, Uncle Nathan hired an engineer to run his factory, but every time Uncle Nathan looked for the engineer he saw him sitting outside, seeming to be just lolling in the sun. Disgusted, Uncle Nathan fired the man. The Kroll brothers—the plumbers turned ice cream men—learning that the engineer was available, immediately hired him for their factory across the street. Soon Uncle Nathan's production started breaking down. Nothing worked right. The Kroll brothers, on the other hand, suddenly had a smooth running operation. And the engineer? He was still sitting outside, enjoying the sun. The Kroll brothers were no dummies. They had realized that the engineer, from his preferred place in the sun, was able to keep his eye on everything. Years later, one of the Kroll brothers wanted to marry me. As I said, they were no dummies.

In the meantime, Lea, who was trying to adjust to her new surroundings, tried her hand at cooking for immigrants in her apartment. Many of her male customers still had families living in Eastern Europe and were saving money to send for them. Eating at Lea's was cheaper than eating in a restaurant.

Because of the hustle and bustle in their apartment, Reuben had no real place to call home. Lea did the cooking in Tillie's kitchen, and because the apartment was so cramped, he was sent to live with his other Aunt Rose, where he slept on two chairs that were pushed together. A woman abandoned by her husband, Aunt Rose had three children of her own. A bitter woman, she mistreated Reuben badly.

In time, Lea was able to rent the apartment on the second floor of her brother's house on Sackman Street. But even there, there was still not a lot of room—Lea and Reuben shared the apartment with Eleanor and Eddie.

Reuben joined the Communist Party in his late teens because they offered free boat rides with young, promiscuous girls who did not hesitate to offer their favors to would-be Party members. When Reuben's formal invitation from the Party arrived, Eddie found it and told Lea. As the unsuspecting Reuben entered the door that night, we could hear the yelling up and down the block. After that, Reuben would never have to worry about a Joe McCarthy or a House Un-American Activities Committee. He was cured by the time Lea—and her broomstick—finished with him.

As time went on, Lea's ad hoc cafeteria allowed her to meet all kinds of people, including Benjamin Elkin, a one-armed day laborer and bachelor. Elkin was smitten with Lea and begged her to marry him. But Lea had other plans and, romantically speaking, he wasn't one of them. Attempting to get closer to her, Elkin offered to invest what little money he had in a business—any business—with her.

When he presented the idea of a business partnership to her, brother Sam suggested they go into the ice cream business, because that was what he knew. He talked them into opening a factory in the Bronx, at the time still virgin "frozen treat" territory. "I'll come up and show you how," he told them.

And so a deal was struck. Lea and Elkin decided to call their new business The Sanitary Ice Cream Company, reflecting Lea's post-typhus concern with health and cleanliness. Fortunately for the business, her poor English and thick accent were incomprehensible to her lawyer, who heard "Senator" instead of "Sanitary." Thus Senator Frozen Products, Inc. was established in 1932, with Lea and Elkin planning to tempt the palates of their clientele— as poor as it was.

From the very start, Lea made it clear that she was in charge. They found a place in the basement of a building on St. Ann's Avenue and 138th Street, near St. Luke's Church in the East Bronx, and made ices in cans, using real lemons and a hand-cranked machine. They paid kids in the neighborhood 25¢ for every batch of lemon ices they turned out.

In the 1920s and early 1930s, the technology required to make ices was pretty straightforward: put ice and salt into large containers and set five- and ten-gallon cans of crushed ice inside. A paddle inside the can was cranked by hand, fruit was added, and the ice was literally turned into sherbet. Lea also froze fruit juices in test tubes and put a wooden dowel down the center to make ice pops.

When Senator's products came out of the freezer and were put into the wagons for delivery, they didn't melt because they were tightly packed with bullets made from an alloy that stayed cold for long periods of time. Until refrigerated trucks came along, there was always the need to "make extra" because things would melt or spoil, but the icy delights from St. Ann's Avenue were slurped up by the Bronx kids who hung out at the corner candy store, and also by their parents who frequented the superettes, the neighborhood grocery stores that carried a little bit of everything.

Reuben was eager to help in any way he could because they only had a limited amount of time in which to make a year's worth of income. You needed to make enough money during your season—in this case, the warm months—to carry you through the winter, when the business was essentially dead. It wasn't that people didn't want to eat ices or ice cream in the winter, it was because there were no home or store freezers in which to store it.

As a result, it was a seasonal product. Once the cold weather came, you couldn't give ice cream away. So during the late fall and winter, Reuben worked for a firm that specialized in antique reproductions and his best friend, Benny Golub, who also worked the summer months at Senator, worked for Western Union.

Starting in late spring, Reuben and Benny would take off after classes at Junior High School 109 (on Dumont Avenue) and ride the subway to the East Bronx, where they'd build their muscles squeezing lemons, hauling salt and cranking out Italian ices. Then the two boys loaded the cans of ices onto horse-drawn wagons that delivered to stores throughout the Bronx.

The ices came in five-gallon containers. Once inside the stores, the boys placed the containers in wooden barrels lined with ice. Then they sprinkled the ice with heavy salt granules. As the ice melted, it kept the lemon ices cold and stiff enough so that it could be scooped into cups.

As the Depression worsened, money became tighter and tighter. Reuben, always aggressive and entrepreneurial, remained a go-getter, constantly looking for ways to make an extra buck. For example, in those days, the only telephone on the block was at the corner candy store. When the phone rang, Reuben took it upon himself to summon the person who was being called. His tip was usually no more than a penny or two, but it was money in hand. In the winter, he shoveled snow for the city for 50¢ an hour. At one point, he sold potatoes he'd baked in fires he built on the streets.

Reuben sold newspapers in the subways, and learned early about the cruelty of prejudice: rival Irish newsboys beat him mercilessly for intruding on what they considered to be their turf. When Lea saw her beaten and bloodied son, she shrugged and asked, "Who told you to go there?" Her goal was for her boy to learn to be strong, and learn he did. And I learned from Lea that it takes a tough, determined woman to turn a boy into a man.

Maybe it was the memory of scrounging around in the garbage that motivated Reuben, but one thing was certain: He had a deep and abiding hunger for success. He was also, in his own way, a loner, deeply private, a dreamer off on the seas of his genius, focused on making something of himself.

In the meantime, Elkin's faith in Lea's abilities was not misplaced. In that first year Lea and Elkin did $10,000 worth of business—a pot full of money for a business that only operated during the summertime.

ℭHAPTER Two

—The dog who stays on the porch will find no bones.

I first noticed Reuben Mattus walking down the street on his way home from work. He was wearing a sweater with holes in the arms, and his look drew me to him. I was only 13 and tall for my age. Because I was also smart, I was able to pass as an older girl. He would wave to me on his way to and from the subway, but we didn't become friends until the night Zeeske, my boyfriend of the moment, pulled shtick I didn't appreciate.

Our crowd used to gather at Rendezvous, a sort of poor man's supper club in the basement of a private house in East Flatbush, a long walk from where we lived. My father was very strict and watched me like a hawk. He always wanted to know where I was, whom I was with, and where I was going. And when I finished junior high school, he made sure I continued on to high school, something rare for Jewish girls from East New York back then. With his encouragement and support, I became self-confident and sure of myself. I was quite popular in school and considered a leader in our social group.

In our neighborhood, when a boy liked a girl, he would show it by asking if he could walk her to Rendezvous. With his pimply face, Zeeske wasn't very good-looking, but he was a singer who attracted girls like flies to honey. He liked me because I was pretty. I was happy to have him walk me to the club because I liked his voice, and I liked having a boyfriend. My sharp sense of humor, which I brought with me from home, allowed me to mingle with the older teens. (I have always said that God gives us a sense of humor as a tool to help us survive.) Other boys from the neighborhood were after me, too. With three brothers in the house, I figured I knew all I needed to know about boys.

One night on our way to the club, Zeeske stopped to talk to two girls, leaving me hanging like a wallflower. I was furious. My father did not raise me to be treated like that. When Zeeske finally returned and asked me to join him, I knew I was going to tell him to get lost. Once at the club, Reuben spotted me sitting by myself and stopped to talk. When I complained about Zeeske, Reuben said with a grin, "Don't worry about it, you're with me now."

On the long walk home, we started talking and talking and talking—it became a conversation that lasted for more than 60 years.

When we reached the corner of Sackman Street, Reuben paused and looked at me. "Why wonder about Zeeske and what he wants?" he asked, with one hand in his pocket and the other spread out in front of him. "The hell with him! I'll take you out! How old are you anyway?"

I smiled sweetly and lied through my teeth. "I'm going to be 16." Well, that wasn't really a lie. I would eventually turn 16.

We got to the front door of my house, where my father was waiting. I introduced them, but my father already knew Reuben was Lea Mattus' son. When Reuben left, my father said to me, "I like that boy. He's going to go places. He's hardworking and he's a good guy. He's the one for you."

He was right. From that moment on, it was Rose and Reuben forever. I was crazy about him. He was so handsome. We fell in love with each other, and that was that. (It was funny that in Yiddish we both had the same name. I was Rivke Rochel and he was Reuven, shortened to Rufke. I always called him Rufky and his friends called him Ruby.)

As the oldest child and the only girl in my family, I had my own room on the ground floor with a large window facing the front. Reuben would invariably knock on it when he returned from the plant in the Bronx at midnight and we would talk for hours. That summer, he got me my first job as a packer at Yukon, earning 10¢ an hour—and I was glad to get it. Eventually he made me another offer, a lifelong one, and I never had a day off thereafter.

Making ice cream has never been a business for softies, and in those early days it was especially difficult. During the season, the process was an exhausting, months-long effort in which people spent day after day, week after week, ankle-deep in freezing saltwater that spilled onto the floor from huge wooden mixing tubs. We'd be engulfed in the overpowering fumes of whatever flavor was being made and on constant alert in order to prevent technical breakdowns that could spoil ingredients or melt the ice cream. In addition to beating cream into frozen products, workers had to play "beat the clock" to prevent the product from melting in the heat.

In spite of the pressure, and the deepening Depression, Lea's business kept people employed. War was brewing in Europe again, and many wonderful, talented people flocked to America in droves during the mid-to-late 1930s. Those already in America were willing to work hard for very little pay, and Lea's workers understood that the only way they could make a living was to make sure she stayed in business.

Many of her workers were professors and engineers who fled the Nazi regime and knew they were lucky to be in America and have jobs. Lea's ten workers put in 12 to 14 hours a day, six days a week, all summer long. There were nights when the factory never shut down, when there were emergencies—like an equipment breakdown, or, happily, a big order that needed to be filled at the last minute. Lea ran a tight ship, pushing herself and those around her.

Like her son after her, Lea was willing to do her part and then some. She met people more than halfway, and most who came to know her developed a deep, abiding respect for her. But she and Reuben didn't always see eye to eye, especially when it came to improving the quality of the ice cream.

Their disagreements were serious and loud, and forced Reuben to refine his ideas about business in general. As he broke free of his mother's attitudes and confirmed his own convictions, he schooled himself in the business that would consume him until the day he died.

He learned to beware of bait-and-switch tactics from salesmen who came to peddle ingredients to Lea: chocolate, powdered eggs, dairy products and containers of all kinds. For example, one day a paunchy guy in a cheap suit showed up to sell Lea vanilla extract. As people busied themselves grinding out ice pops, a worker directed the salesman to the boss, who was wearing a long apron and knee-high rubber boots.

Lea had never seen him before. When he handed her a sample bottle, she brought it to her nose, sniffed it, rubbed some of the liquid onto her hands and brought her palms up to her nose, taking a deep whiff to judge the quality of the vanilla. The aroma filled the air and was noticed by people several feet away.

"Well," she finally admitted, "it's not too bad. How much do you want for it?"

"That'll be $5 a gallon, Mrs. Mattus," the salesman told her, pulling an order pad from his sample box.

She raised her eyebrows and took a long look at him. "I won't spend $5 for this!" she barked, as if the very thought was ridiculous, and turned back to her table. They haggled on a price, eventually settling for $1.50 for

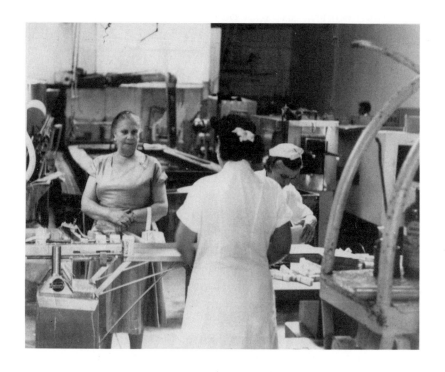

Lea at the factory.

a gallon. The salesman's company, of course, delivered a much cheaper product—much paler, a bland shadow of the original. Lea couldn't have been blind to the difference, but she didn't care. To her, the variation in quality between a superior ingredient and one similar to it in name only wasn't worth the extra money. So she haggled down ingredient prices to improve her profit margins, and had help from her plant manager, who arranged a few kickbacks for himself in the process. The net result was ice cream that was barely edible. To her son's chagrin, that remained her way of doing business, and the cheap ice cream she made still sold in the summertime, enabling her to make a decent living for her children.

Lea spent long days and many nights at the factory, standing at the packing tables side by side with the girls, working as hard and as fast as they, if not harder. The ice cream might have been fourth-rate, but no one ever questioned Lea's personal integrity or the advice she graciously handed out.

My family was involved in business, as well. My Uncle Nathan owned a tailor shop in The Hub of the Bronx, at Third Avenue and 149th Street. The main post office was located on one corner, the banks had branches within blocks of each other, and all sorts of businesses plied their trades there.

Nathan was short, dark, and somewhat stocky with a full head of hair that remained until the day he died. To me he always looked a little like Napoleon, but he had considerable integrity as a person and a businessman, which I admired. Around Christmas 1933, Uncle Nathan asked for my help because he thought I had a head for business. He liked me because I was attractive and outgoing and felt I would make a good salesperson.

"I've been watching traffic down at The Hub for weeks—plenty of people out there, looking for gifts this time of year. I could make ties, and you could sell them. We can get a storefront by the month. Would you like to become partners with me?" he asked.

It was an offer I couldn't refuse. We went looking for a store, trying to keep the rent down as much as possible. We found an empty key shop, six feet by 15 feet, with a window facing Third Avenue, costing us $50 a month for three months. Nathan figured he could hang a curtain to divide the space in two—use the rear to make the ties and use the front to sell them at the princely sum of a quarter each.

We whitewashed the shop, and Nathan put up display racks. He used salvaged fabrics that made handsome ties, which he pressed and hung on the racks. But the ties did not move. They looked too expensive and the display was too fancy. People strolled in, browsed and maybe picked out a single tie that they'd want a nice gift box for, and straggled out again—all for a quarter. I quickly realized we were going to die like that. I wanted a crowd, not one person at a time; a crowd draws other people.

"I have an idea. I have a table at home," I said. "Let's go get it."

"A table? What for?" he asked.

"You'll see," I replied.

We jumped into his old Ford with a hole in the roof and no heater. (It wasn't meant to be a convertible, but a cherry bomb dropped by my brothers had blown a hole through the top on the previous Fourth of July.) We grabbed the table—a small kitchen table, four feet by three feet, with a gray marbleized top and tubular legs—and brought it to the shop.

I took a few cardboard boxes from the back and put them on the table. Then I yanked those beautifully pressed ties off the display racks and threw them every which way into the boxes. On the window I taped a big sign in bold letters that said: Sale! Sale! Four for One Dollar!

My Uncle Nathan was yelling at me nonstop while I set myself up.

"What are you doing?" he yelled. "I spent all night pressing those ties."

"Do you want to keep them or do you want to sell them?" I replied.

Within the hour, half a dozen people gathered out front and were picking their way through the boxes. Soon, more folks stopped to look—wouldn't you? In short order, I created a run on the market. We unloaded our entire inventory and kept selling ties as fast as Nathan could produce them. I gave customers only one box for every four ties, and some bought several boxfuls.

By the time I graduated from high school, I was secretary of my class and Reuben was my steady. I will never forget the day he introduced me to his mother. I was terrified of her. I know it was a Friday, because the rabbi came to empty the *pushke*, and Lea always stayed home on Friday to prepare for the Sabbath. As we walked up the stairs, Reuben told me not to be afraid. His sister, Eleanor, would be there, too.

Lea was standing and did not invite me to sit down. "Mama, I want you to meet the girl I like," Reuben said. Her laser-like blue eyes looked me over.

"You like her?" she asked him.

He answered, "This is my girlfriend. Yes, of course I like her. That's why I brought her up here."

"Well," she retorted, "You like her, I like her."

At the end of my senior year, my friends and I were standing on Bushwick Avenue when Reuben drove up in his friend Ziggy's yellow roadster, with the top down. "My mother wants to see you," he said to me.

I hopped into the car and made sure he drove past all my girlfriends. Reuben was the only fellow in my crowd who drove, and I wanted to show off. When we arrived at the apartment, Lea was sitting sternly at the head of the dining room table with four diamond rings in front of her. "Take your pick," she said to me.

I was speechless, and asked her to pick the ring. She insisted I choose, and I pointed to a one-and-one-half carat diamond. I went to hug and kiss her, but Lea remained stiff. Reuben put the ring on my finger and we headed off to show my parents and then my friends. He drove right

Rose Vesel Mattus

VESEL, ROSE
429 Sackman Street
*Another maiden of Lane
Who hasn't acquired much
fame.*
Bus. Practice, Sten Speed,
Comm. Law Clubs; Sec. Mr.
Aaronson; Basketball Team.
Business

Franklin K. Lane High School Yearbook with
inscription from Reuben (1935).

into the middle of the crowd at the high school. I remember thinking, "How lucky could I be?" I walked around like my wrist was broken as I showed off my ring.

My parents were thrilled. They loved Reuben and they were overjoyed because I was so happy.

Reuben and I were to be married in March 1936, before the ice cream season began. My parents wanted to make a real wedding, but there wasn't enough money. To my father, the idea of his only daughter marrying without a proper ceremony and a *seudat mitzvah*, the traditional wedding feast, was too painful to consider. So he decided to borrow the money from The Morris Plan Company, a Jewish lending firm, but I put a quick stop to that. How would he, a poor tailor who picked up odd jobs whenever they were available, be in a position to pay it back? The debt would inevitably become mine, and I wanted to save every penny to buy Reuben a delivery truck. I was adamant that a one-day luxury wedding would not interfere with our long-term plans.

My father resolved to talk to Lea. He reasoned it was her son's wedding, too. Maybe she would agree to split the expenses. Lea listened politely and then got up and said, "I don't make no weddings. The groom's family pays for the ring. The bride's family pays for the wedding." Lea had made up her mind.

There would be no wedding in March because, in the end, there was no money. Instead we waited two more months and decided to get married on May 9.

The ceremony was held in Rabbi Morris Tomacheff's study in Brooklyn. We invited very few people to the ceremony, and we planned no wedding feast. My father was devastated, but what could we do? Just before the wedding, Reuben gave me $25 in cash and told me to buy myself something pretty. I found a lovely gray-and-maroon dress and a little hat with shoes to match.

In the meantime, Lea was outraged. We were getting married right in the middle of the ice cream season.

"Are you crazy?" she asked. "How can I leave the plant?"

She didn't. The wedding was delayed for two hours because Reuben had to finish his deliveries. After the ceremony, my husband and I went to the Dog Face Chinese Restaurant on Pitkin Avenue where, for about 50¢, we ate to our hearts' content. When the truck from the ice cream plant arrived, we finished our wedding meal and picked up Popsicles from Big Bear in Brooklyn to bring to Senator in the Bronx. Wedding or no wedding, business came first.

Even though I didn't have a traditional Jewish wedding with all the trimmings, I did get to have my picture taken in a wedding gown. Six months after Reuben and I were married, our friend Ben Golub walked down the aisle with his wonderful wife, Anne. They had a big, beautiful traditional Jewish wedding, and Anne eagerly shared her good fortune with us. She had me rent a wedding gown and Reuben a tux, and when they had their pictures taken, they also took our portrait. Both wedding pictures—the original with me in the lovely outfit that I bought with the money Reuben gave me and the "official wedding portrait" taken the following November—sit on my night table to this very day.

Rose and Reuben's wedding picture.

Anne Golub, Rose Haber and Rose (1936).

ℭHAPTER Three

—Do not accept the acceptable.

Senator was always a modest success. To keep up with the business' growth, Elkin invested more of his own money in equipment, vats, cans and mixing machines. And so, by the mid-1930s when the plant on St. Ann's Avenue became too small, Senator moved to a larger facility at 510 Southern Boulevard in the South Bronx. The beige brick building had huge windows that allowed light to pour in and occupied about 10,000 square feet. It had space for a "hardening room" and a large walk-in freezer where the finished product could be stored until it was needed for delivery.

Just before World War II, Reuben and I settled at 500 Southern Boulevard, right next to the new plant. I was pregnant with our first child, Natalie, and worked as a bookkeeper in the factory.

Lea continued to commute from Brooklyn. Reuben

wanted to send a car service to take her to and from work, but she would have none of it.

"I like the subway," she told him. "They open the doors for me, and then they close the doors for me. What do I need with a car service?" Besides, she only had to walk half a block from the subway to the plant, and she loved the work, especially being with the girls at the factory.

Right after we were married, in order to buy Reuben a truck to make his deliveries, I went to the First National City Bank across the street from the factory to secure a $3,000 loan. Since Senator had its account there, as did I—my little savings account into which I made my weekly deposits—the bank manager gave me the loan.

It was the height of the Depression, and we worked around the clock in the summer, three shifts a day. Reuben worked the night shift with the German refugees.

We were known as an ice cream novelty house: pops, sandwiches, fudgesicles, and the like. One of Reuben's real hits was a half-pint container we called "Big Shot." It consisted of a portion of vanilla ice cream flanked by two slabs of orange sherbet. Long before Häagen-Dazs, it was Reuben's most successful product. It put Senator on the map. Another reason Senator was successful was because we bought cheap and sold cheap: Ices sold for 2¢ each; pops were 3¢.

But honest businessmen were not the only ones in the Bronx trying to make money in the ice cream industry. In the 1930s gangsters roamed the Bronx looking to shake down ice cream factories, trying to steal a share of other people's hard-earned success. These were small-time hoodlums who would go from one factory to another, trying to extort protection money from owners. If you didn't give them what they wanted, they would flip over your delivery trucks or do other damage. Once they stink-bombed the Berke Cake Company and ruined their stock. When bums such as these showed up, a wave of genuine fear would surge through the small-time business people.

One morning, a couple of these toughs showed up in front of our plant. I had just come back to the factory from the bank and was surprised to see a shiny black LaSalle with two men inside pulling up to the entrance way. One was young, slightly built, in a double-breasted suit and a broad-brimmed fedora; the other was a burly guy with a square face and maybe ten years older. The younger hood pointed at Carlo, a string bean of a Hispanic who worked for us on the loading dock and yelled, "Hey, you. We wanna see da boss."

Carlo dropped the 100lb. sack of sugar he was carrying on his shoulder and ran to get Lea. I walked past the car and slipped through the front door. Carlo was yelling "Mrs. Mattus! Mrs. Mattus!" with some despe-ration, but she was oblivious, working the line. When she finally heard him, she became annoyed. "Vat you vant? I'm busy." He told her about the waiting men.

Lea grabbed a broom on her way out the door, as if she were planning to swat a rat. She squinted at the thugs, who were leaning against the LaSalle as if they owned the street. The little guy pulled himself off the car and adjusted his shoulders and swaggered. Lea lifted the broom and swung hard.

"You get out of here, you gangsters, you!" she yelled before he could even open his mouth. She was hysterical with fury. "You don't leave here right now, I'm calling the District Attorney, you hear? The District Attorney!" (In those days, when a merchant in the Bronx called the District Attorney, he came and something happened.)

Waving her broom, she took another step toward them, glared, and cursed: "Your wives should be widows and wear boots like me and stand in the wet!"

The short hood stared at her; the big guy still in the car, kept his eyes locked on the steering wheel. Shorty sneered at Lea, rubbed his nose, and casually slipped into the car. They drove off and we never heard from them again. Other ice cream companies may have paid protec-tion money, but we never did.

Before Reuben and I were married, Lea's bookkeeper was Harry Kaplan, a medium-size man with a mustache who looked like the actor John Gilbert. He offered to teach me as much as he could about the business. He left after Reuben and I were married, and my sister-in-law, Marion, my brother Al's wife, came to pitch in with the book-keeping.

I may have been the bookkeeper, but when I was needed on the production line I'd go out on the floor. There was always the threat of an emergency because the goods were so perishable. If a girl didn't show up, someone had to take her place or there would be spoilage. "Rose," they'd holler, and I'd go running from March to late September, when the business would slowly grind to a halt.

One winter, when the factory was closed, I took a job as a bookkeeper in a Brooklyn commercial bakery owned by gangsters. When I went for my interview, I met with one of the plant's accountants. After we spoke, he called the senior owner, Johnny Andosco, over to meet me. Andosco recognized my name.

"You come from the Bronx?" he asked.

"Yes, I do."

He studied me for a moment. "You know a Mrs. Mattus in the Bronx?"

"She's my mother-in-law."

"Oh," he said knowingly. "How is Mama?"

Two minutes later I had the job at the unheard-of salary of $15.00 per week. Men with families were lucky to be making half of that.

I still don't know if the plant racketeers were the same goodfellas who tried to shake down Lea, but if they weren't, they sure knew who she was.

One of the products prepared in the factory was the charlotte russe, a confection you don't see too much any-more. In this plant, cake arrived from a bakery in a flat pan. With a cookie cutter, a worker would slice the cake into small circles, then 20 or so girls placed the cake into special cardboard, circular scalloped cups. Men with decorator bags then squeezed whipped cream onto the cake and, as the coup de grâce, a maraschino cherry was placed on top. The complete charlotte russes were then packed 24 in a box that distributors then sold.

The plant also made jelly apples. Apples would be speared with a pointed stick, dipped in boiling jelly that hardened to a mirror-like finish, and then placed on trays filled with coconut. As the jelly hardened, the coconut would stick and provide a white crown upon which the apples could rest as they were displayed. Both the apples and charlotte russes were popular items, sold primarily during the winter. In the summer's heat they would have dissolved into a melted mess.

In order to get to work on time, I crawled out of our warm bed at 4 A.M., the blackest, coldest hour of the night. It was cold, but, in those days, the subways were safe.

The other girls at the plant worked in the bakery during the day, but many of them stayed on at night well past working hours. They moonlighted by partying with fellows who either worked at the plant or owned it. The racketeers who owned the factory loved fooling around as much as they loved making money. I was no Goody-Two-Shoes, but this was too much for me. I avoided the back room like the plague and took my lunch down to the corner cafeteria.

One of the seedier characters at the plant was Eddie, a Jewish partner. He stalked me whenever I tried to leave the shop to invite me into the back room. I told him my husband was all the party I needed and I was going home to him. Eventually, his constant harassment proved too much for me. Even though I feared losing my job, I told my boss at work about it. I never saw Eddie again.

Around Christmas time, after I'd been working at the plant for a few months, Andosco invited me to attend a party he was throwing for everyone at the local Chinese restaurant. When I turned him down, there was a heavy silence. For a long and uncomfortable moment I was sure I was going to be fired. Losing that $15 per week would have killed Reuben and me.

Finally, he smiled and threw a piece of paper at me—a $100 bill. He said he knew the subway was really cold at 4 A.M. "Go buy yourself a warm coat," he ordered.

"Mr. Andosco," I said, "you pay me a good salary, and I don't want any extra money."

"You're a good lady, Rose. Go get yourself the coat."

And I did just that. I bought my first fur, a black seal coat for $75. It kept me nice and warm for the rest of the winter—and 60 years later, I still own it!

With the ice cream factory shuttered for winter, Reuben got a job for Interboro News in Washington Heights. Interboro News operated the newsstands adjacent to subway station entrances and on station platforms.

Interboro was a tough company to work for. If an employee working the stand was shortchanged by a customer, or if someone lifted something from the stand, management held the worker responsible—and charged him retail price for whatever was taken. The policy meant that people often went home without their pay and owed their bosses money from the following week's salary. Reuben spent lots of time helping his co-workers reclaim their stolen property, earning himself the respect and admiration of his peers.

I will never forget the time Reuben went into work one morning and found a bag full of money that was supposed to have been dropped down the company's chute the night before. Every evening, when Interboro workers went off shift, they were supposed to place their daily receipts into a bag that was marked with the worker's identifying number. The bag was then dropped down a chute to be retrieved by the company.

When Reuben found the bag that morning, he could have pocketed everything in it, or, if he wanted to use the opportunity to get in good with management, he could have reported finding the bag. Instead, he tracked down the fellow who had worked the stand the previous evening and told him about the bag. Reuben then dropped the bag down the chute himself and no one in management was the wiser.

But the fellow whose job Reuben had saved was so overcome with gratitude that he told all their fellow employees what had happened and what a wonderful man Reuben Mattus was.

As a natural leader, Reuben organized the men and listed their grievances in a letter to management. When the owners discovered what he was up to, they invited him to join the ranks of management—with a substantial increase in salary—if he would report his fellow workers who they considered troublemakers. This he refused to do, because to him being a stool pigeon was as serious a sin as eating on Yom Kippur (a fast day and one of the holiest days of the Jewish year).

Though not observant in the religious sense, Reuben and I were always concerned about the welfare of others and passionately concerned about the fate of the Jewish people. Well before the 1940s, Reuben foresaw the terrible fate that awaited the Jews of Europe. We spent hour upon hour trying to raise money among our people in the United States. Through the years, we met with some real success in these endeavors, but we also learned what it felt like to have doors slammed in our faces. Reuben and I couldn't understand how people who had been blessed could turn their backs on those who were suffering. Even when we had next to nothing, we always made sure to give a certain percentage of what little we did have to charity, even more so when summer came and things were good.

And it wasn't just people that benefited from our feelings for others. One day, Reuben discovered a mangy dog hanging out in front of the Bronx plant. It was in pitiful condition, literally shaking in its tracks. Reuben took the dog in, fed it and nurtured it back to health. When it was well, he gave it to one of the guys at the plant and made him promise to take care of it. Whenever the worker brought the dog around, it would always run to Reuben.

41

Reuben came by his charitable nature honestly. His mother was a very charitable woman, a real—as they say in Hebrew—*Aishes Chayil*. Whether our season was good or only fair, she insisted on giving the same amount to charity. Why should the poor suffer because we'd had a lousy season? I remember once asking her after a particularly bad week how she could still give her usual amount of charity? "God will help us," she responded, and darned if the season didn't turn around.

In 1934, Ben Elkin finally despaired of ever convincing Lea to say yes to his proposal of marriage. Instead, he found Hilda, whom he married and brought to the plant to work.

Although Lea did not want Elkin as a husband for herself, she certainly was not pleased that he had cast his eyes elsewhere. I don't know if it was a simple case of jealousy, but for whatever the reason, Lea did not want the new Mrs. Elkin to have anything to do with the factory.

The animosity between Lea and the Elkins soon reached fever pitch, and my mother-in-law became unreasonable. She refused to allow her erstwhile partner to draw more than a token salary, forcing him and his new wife to live off meager savings.

Toward the end of the season in 1936, after Reuben and I were married, Elkin called me at the office to ask if I could see him at home.

"I've been in the hospital, Rose," he said softly.

Poor Elkin had never done anything to me. "I'll come over during lunchtime," I promised.

"I want to talk about selling some shares I've got in the business. To you and Rufky...on the quiet," he added, using the pet name reserved for only those closest to Reuben.

It was a miserable day, cold and raining, with a chill that went right through you. I kept slipping on the soggy leaves that hadn't been cleaned as I made my way to the Elkin's fourth floor walk-up apartment on Simpson Street, around the corner from the Senator plant.

Chocolat-Menier Convention in Cleveland.

Top: Uncle Nathan of Big Bear (5th from left).
Bottom: Eddie Lipitz and Benjamin Elkin
(2nd and 3rd from left).

Elkin opened the door of the dingy apartment and smiled when he saw me. He looked awful. In the relativelyshort time he had been in the business, Elkin had become an old man with white hair and a tired shuffle.

He invited me into the kitchen for a cup of coffee, and after a few minutes of small talk about the plant we fell silent, not knowing how to begin this discussion.

I started. "Why do you want to sell the shares, Ben?" I asked quietly.

He knew I had not come to his home to hurt him. He lit a cigarette and fiddled with the match before dropping it into the ashtray. "I need the money," he admitted, without elaborating or looking at me. "They're eight shares, Rose, and they're worth $475.00 apiece. But I don't want anybody to know."

I did the calculation in my head: $3,800. It might as well have been a million. We didn't have it. But since when did that ever stop me? "I'll let you know as soon as I have it," I told him.

I walked back into the cold in a state of shock. I had to talk to Reuben.

As soon as I reached the plant, I pulled Reuben aside and told him Elkin wanted sell us his shares immediately. "We have to get the money to pay him, but we have to keep it quiet. Lea can't know," I said.

It wasn't asking a lot of Reuben to keep this from his mother. They were in the midst of one of their not-so-unusual arguments, and, at the moment, were not speaking. As the daughter-in-law, I wasn't going to get in the middle of that. And besides, there were Elkin's feelings to consider.

Reuben looked at me the way he always did when questions about money arose. I was his best and most trusted financial partner. Every night, the minute he walked through the door, he would empty his pockets on the little table in the front hall. It was my job to take that money to the bank to deposit it into our account. Reuben was the kind of guy who never knew if he even had money in his pocket. When he went out shopping, he often had to hand over his watch until he could show up with cash to cover his purchases.

"You want to get the shares?" he whispered back. It really wasn't a question. "Do it."

I nodded, picked up my handbag, and walked across the street to the First National City Bank. The dismal weather hadn't let up, and now there was even a colder wind blowing.

I explained to the manager what Reuben and I wanted to do, and the manager, who knew a good business investment when he saw one, handed over the cash almost immediately. I then went to see Elkin. I gave him the $3,800 and he signed his shares over. Suddenly, we were part owners of Senator, even though Lea was still the boss and did not have a clue as to what we had done.

The tension between Reuben and his mother was certainly not all Lea's fault. Today we would say they had irreconcilable differences. They didn't see eye to eye when it came to business. She was interested in making money by paying out as little as possible and charging as low a price as she could get away with. He wanted to improve the quality of the product and make money by creating a demand for it.

Without inner strength and resilience, it was hard to survive around Reuben or his mother. He gave 100% of himself and expected no less from anyone else. A perfectionist, he insisted that his product had to be mixed, handled and sold correctly.

Because he cared so much, Reuben brought out the best in his people. He had a real flair for designing workspace and managing time. Years later, it became clear the Häagen-Dazs' success was based on the standards and devotion lavished on the product by Reuben Mattus. This demand for quality often put him at odds with his mother, who cared only about the bottom line and did not like the idea of anyone—not even her beloved son—interfering in the way she ran the business.

Eventually, of course, Reuben told Lea about our eight shares from Elkin, and she signed over eight more shares to us as a gift. But despite gestures like that and temporary lulls in their arguments, I knew eventually Lea and Reuben were going to reach a point of no return.

It happened when Reuben was serving as Senator's outside man, handling sales and deliveries. Reuben was constantly insisting that an improved product would improve business. Lea believed in her profit margins, and for her there was no proof like the proof you took to the bank.

Reuben's instinct was correct, but he couldn't prove it until Eddie, one of his best customers, gave him the proof he needed. An avuncular Irishman, Eddie owned a corner candy store with school supplies and penny candy on one side and a soda fountain on the other. He sold malts, egg creams, ice cream sodas and made-to-order sundaes.

The store was on the corner of Beck Street and Southern Boulevard, and Eddie steadily bought all the ice cream novelties we turned out, but not our bulk ice cream in the two-and-a-half gallon containers. Eddie was content to use Horton's and Breyers products.

Finally, Reuben asked him why he wouldn't buy Senator. "If you buy five two-and-half gallon cans from me every week, it'll save you enough money to pay your rent here," Reuben told him, knowing Eddie was paying much more for the big companies' ice cream. Reuben was willing to sell him Senator for next to nothing.

Eddie was interested. "Okay," he agreed. "Send me five cans."

A few weeks later, on perhaps the hottest, muggiest day of the year, Reuben showed up at Eddie's, hoping to land a huge order for the rest of the season. He was in for a rude awakening. Eddie took him aside, sat him down and said, "Listen, Ruby, listen carefully. I know what you want. You're a good kid, and I like you. And believe me, I'll sell any novelty you put in that freezer out front. But forget about those cans you sent me. Forget about them. They're pure shit. If you gave them to me for nothing, I wouldn't take them."

Reuben was shocked. That night, as he dumped his change on the table by the door, he told me what had happened. "I don't know what the hell is going on in that plant, but I've got to get in there," he muttered.

Reuben hit the books, though he was not an educated man. With my high school diploma, I had more formal education than he did. But Reuben had a reverential respect for books and academic learning, and approached problems like a scholar. "There are no problems," he liked to say, "only solutions."

He now went to the library and checked out all the books he could find about ice cream. One night he looked up from one of the books and barked, "I can't understand how we can put a hose in the batch, and just leave it there. According to the book, it's not the right thing to do."

Reuben earned a stationary engineer's license (just by studying on his own) and became an expert at understanding the mechanical functions of the equipment in the factory and how people used them. He learned fast, and when he compared what was in the books to what was going on in his mother's plant, it drove him into a fury. There was nothing remotely scientific about Senator's selection of ingredients or mixing methods. No one measured ingredients and no one kept production records. People working for Senator accepted bribes from suppliers right under Lea's nose. Hoses twisted and flopped around the main manufacturing space, tripping people. The floor was awash in frigid saltwater overflow, and people sloshed around in galoshes, pushing the slush back and forth with brooms and mops.

The books Reuben read described the importance of maintaining a tightly organized work environment, using precise measurements to assure a reliable product with a stable consistency and taste. Taste, above all, was important to Reuben. He wanted to give the public something more than his mother's "cold and sweet stuff."

Of course, Lea was not amused. Since 1932 she'd been working like crazy to keep the wolves from the door, and her formula had worked for a decade. But Reuben finally cornered her in the back office one hot afternoon and told her how he wanted to change the business. I sat there, nervous, waiting for the coming explosion. Lea thought he was out of his mind and said so.

"And if you think," she added, "that I'm going to throw my hard-earned business into the toilet because you got some cockamamie idea you want to try out, you got another think coming. We did fine all these years without your fancy ideas."

"Did fine?" he shouted back. "You got people out there," he yelled, "who won't touch our bulk-pack ice cream because it's garbage. They can't give it away!"

"You can't please everybody," she concluded, and folded her arms across her chest with a hurt but defiant grimace on her face. Reuben sighed. In the post-explosion silence, I could hear the neighborhood kids playing stickball through the open window.

"You don't understand!" he said in frustration, pulling out a cigarette and starting to puff. It seemed to calm him down a little. "You came up here to the Bronx to start a business. Uncle Sam shows you the ropes, but even he didn't know much about what he was doing. Elkin, a good man, was a complete greenhorn, so he let you do things your way. And your way is, 'If it ain't cheap as borscht, forget about it.'" He took another drag on his cigarette, let the smoke out slowly, and leaned forward on his elbows. "You chisel here, you chisel there."

"What chisel, Rufky? Don't be foolish. You're talking our profits!"

"But Ma," he countered, "you can't make the business grow like this. We have to build a customer base, people who trust the product, people who can count on it, be loyal to us...."

"Loyal?" she practically shrieked, cutting him off. Her steel blue eyes went dark and wide. "Whadda ya wanna do, marry the customers?" She looked at me and let loose a short, brittle laugh. Reuben, exasperated, turned to me, "Rose, make her see what I mean, will ya?"

Reuben had frequently sought to put me between himself and his mother, to use me as a source of reason when all else failed between them. In the middle of some of their battles, Reuben, in frustration, would put his fist through a wall. But when their rage intensified, I took it as my cue to leave; this was a war I wanted no part of because there was no way to be on the winning side. Once Reuben beseeched me, "Why don't you just tell her off?" I answered without having to think. "Because I'm only her daughter-in-law. You are her son. She will forgive you no matter what you say or do, but not me."

On this particular date, in spite of my better judgment, I took the bait. "All he's saying, Mom," I said, choosing my words very carefully, like picking peaches from a fruit stand, "is that he wants to make ice cream he doesn't have to be ashamed of. He wants to make ice cream he can be proud of. When his customers tell him our ice cream isn't what it should be, it affects him personally."

Lea looked down at her desk, cluttered with papers and bills, the open ledger laying right on top of the pile, and then threw me a sideways glance. "Yeah, I know. My Ruby is a very sensitive young man," and made it sound like Ruby was suffering from some kind of disease. "The trouble is, he'll throw away all my hard-earned money. On what?" And then her sharp-edged sarcasm got the better of her again. "This is ice cream we're talking about, not steak!"

The furious arguments raged on for weeks. I dreaded going in to work. There were tense silences and occasionally quiet moments of reasoned conversation. I never knew what to expect from either of them. But one thing was sure, we worked backbreaking hours to make the season a success, and it was hard to keep our minds focused on anything but immediate problems: meeting delivery deadlines, paying the bills and making sure our trucks got where they had to go without the inevitable meltdowns.

Finally, Reuben had enough and quit the family business, getting a job at Huber's Ice Cream in Connecticut. We were a young family in the Bronx during those hectic years. Natalie had been born in 1939, named for Reuben's father, Nathan. Doris followed two years later, named for my father, David.

After three months, I had enough being alone with the kids in the Bronx and facing Lea in the plant. Reuben knew he had to come back to his family but wouldn't stay in the factory. He bought a truck, put it in my name, and started his own ice cream business called Colony Club Ice Cream. I was the sole owner so that Lea couldn't get her hands on it.

Ruby drove the truck and got customer feedback as he built his route. He bought a second truck, hired his first driver and realized that if he wanted to grow the business he had to fix the production line.

Colony Club helped us build a distribution network in the tri-state area, which later gave us a chance to build up Häagen-Dazs. Reuben began to understand then that the one key to the ice cream business was controlling the distribution.

Eventually Lea began to see things Reuben's way and allowed him to make a few changes. His anger had registered with her and she knew he was the future of the business. As soon as he could, Reuben tinkered with ingredients to improve flavor and texture and, for the first time, established some production standards. He rearranged the machinery on the production floor and studied ways to improve efficiency.

Lea's shop was always clean, but by the time Reuben—who was personally fastidious—finished setting rules and regulations, you could eat off the floor. He laid out money for better flavorings, and paid much closer attention to production values—for example, how long it took to freeze the product and the temperatures involved. He learned that everything affected the taste and texture of ice cream, and if the manufacturer controlled the elements of production, the ice cream came out better. At the same time, he looked to expand his distribution.

One of our marketing techniques was to take a carload of ice cream packed in dry ice with us to parades or the beaches. He'd say, "You can't salute the flag without an ice cream in your other hand, Rose!"

Once we'd reach our destination, we'd park and Reuben would take a box of ice cream with him, while I watched the car. He'd work the street long enough to finish a box, hand me the money, and grab another box. Reuben was only worried that the cops would catch him selling ice cream without a permit, so he did the legwork and I held the money. We would manage to sell everything in the trunk and head home with a pocketbook full of money for the bank.

Lea soon realized that the numbers were improving, and we started spending more money on Reuben's inventive ideas. I know because I wrote the checks—and had to find the money to cover them.

One day in the late 1940s, while riding on the subway, Reuben was struck with a revolutionary concept. He decided it would be a good idea to put refrigerated ice cream vending machines containing ice cream pops and Dixie Cups on New York City Transit Authority subway platforms. By the time he got home, he was just busting to share it with me.

"Think about it, honey. There you are—it's a hot day— you're waiting for the train to come, and a nice ice cream pop or a Dixie Cup is staring you in the face. All you have to do is throw some coins into a slot and take your ice cream. I think they'd sell like hotcakes! What do you think? You with me?"

I threw my arms around him. "I'm always with you Rufky." But I cautioned, "That sounds like a big piece of change, you know?"

Reuben didn't want to spend all of his time with the vending machine idea, so he looked for someone who would go into the venture with him. We knew a salesman by the name of Al Yakira, who worked for the Harlem Paper Co., a company run by reliable people with whom we did lots of business. A tall, good-looking blond with gray eyes and finely cut features, Yakira was always well-dressed in a suit and tie. Al liked Reuben because he was an idea factory as well as an ice cream maker and Al was always looking for ways to make some extra money.

Soon after we talked, Reuben approached Al about the vending machine idea and told him how worried I was about financing it. Reuben was realistic enough to know he needed a bank to work with him and Al said he had one. Al went on: "Look, Ruby, I'll tell you what. I'll handle the finances. I'll go into business with Rose. I'll get the money and we'll pay it off."

Al "handled the financing" of our new vending machine company by applying for a loan at Royal National Bank on 149th Street and Third Avenue. The bank president, William Goldfine, had built his bank into a business-friendly institution with several branches throughout the city. Goldfine was a philanthropic sort and possessed real strength of character. He was a local banker and business-man who knew all his business neighbors and worked with them.

Al and Goldfine made the arrangements, with the bank holding the notes on the equipment—$40,000 worth. I signed the notes with Al and we opened a company called Vendamatic with Al, Reuben and me as principals. We located a company called Revco that sold the compact refrigerated machine we were looking for and could be adapted to suit our needs. In no time, we'd sunk a small fortune into buying, installing and stocking the machines. As Reuben had figured, the pops started selling on the subway platforms.

A few months after we started—the vending machines were turning into a good off-season draw—a kid came by, stuck his arm into one of the machines to steal a pop and got his hand trapped. In short order, we had a lawsuit on our hands. And once the machines started breaking down from old age, we discovered we couldn't get parts to fix them. Al, in the meantime, took off for California. We finally had to junk the whole idea. Then I got a call from the bank.

Since Reuben never got involved with money matters, I went to see Goldfine. I thought about what I could offer Goldfine if he cut me a little slack. By the time I got off the bus on Third Avenue, I had it figured out.

He showed me the note for $40,000 with about $14,000 still outstanding on the loan. Because we were incorporated I could have taken the easy way out and not admitted any obligation—a corporation, a legal entity under the law, would have been the liable "person" in the deal. But that wasn't a good way to establish a relationship with a financial institution.

Goldfine said, "I'm not in the vending business, and I certainly don't want the machines."

"We've closed down the business," I said handing him a check for $3,000, "but my name is on that note, and my name is the only thing that's worth something to me. I'm going to do my best to give you the rest, Mr. Goldfine. We're not rich people, but we have integrity. By the way, I'm not going to pay any more interest on the loan."

A year later, our local bank, Public National, was taken over by Banker's Trust and the new people looked at our operation and refused to extend the $10,000 in credit we usually received to carry us over the winter. I decided to see Goldfine, whose note we had paid off a few months earlier.

After the usual pleasantries, I said, "Mr. Goldfine, I have a little problem."

"Well, sit down and talk to me," he offered.

"I need money...."

"Money? Why don't you bring your account here, and I'll see what we can do for you?"

Because Public National had been across the street from the factory, it had been convenient for our banking needs. To get to Goldfine's bank I'd have to take a bus. But if I needed to change our account to Goldfine's bank to get the money to carry us through the winter, then a

Rose and Lea in the Bronx.

bus ride I'd have to take. Because of the relationship I had established with him, we got the money.

A few years later, when our business had grown some, I approached Goldfine with another idea concerning butterfat, a key ingredient in ice cream. We used butterfat to stabilize milk quality. Our butter vendor was William Menzer, a reliable, old-fashioned businessman who believed in service. He'd deliver 30 or so 40-pound blocks of butter at a time at market price, and he would allow us to owe him the money—in other words, he carried us. Menzer would borrow from his own bank as well, and had to pay his loan off every March, or he couldn't get the money to give us credit.

I told Godlfine I had a chance to bring in fat from Wisconsin and New Zealand, a container load at a time. The New Zealand fat looked like cream. Wisconsin fat was a dairy by-product that was lighter in color, and there were various grades, but these two types of butterfat were the best of the best. I could do well on the price if we bought in huge quantities, and the resulting ice cream would be of superior quality.

"If the bank could make money off that container of butterfat, and if I could, too, wouldn't that be a good deal for us both?

"I bring in a container of butterfat, I get volume and I save money. But we have to pay for it in cash: $100,000. If you can loan me the money, we warehouse the load and you hold the warehouse receipt. I can't get to the butterfat until you release it to me, so when I need it, I give you money."

Eventually, he agreed to give us 80 percent of the financing, and I had to find the other $20,000. I pawned my diamond, my sister-in-law, Eleanor, gave me $8,000, and I found the rest somehow, including taking money from the business. I had to show Goldfine I was responsible. It was March by then; April was coming and our season was about to start.

Goldfine made good money on that loan interest and

we came out way ahead because we paid much less for the fat. As our business relationship improved, Goldfine and I became good friends. And every time a new load of butterfat came in, he put in more money and there was greater volume involved. We sent him other customers, too. Later, I even bought some shares in Goldfine's bank, and so wound up making a little money, as it were, on my own loan.

Being in the ice cream business always meant working with suppliers who were not interested in our grand plans. If you could pay upon delivery or within a short period of time, you could usually get a better price for supplies. Unfortunately, we weren't in that kind of position.

Our 30-quart cans of skim milk, for instance, came from Sam Miller at Queensboro Farms in Long Island City. One summer, his nephew, Harvey, took over and started threatening me that he'd stop making shipments. We'd had a bad season, owed him a lot of money and our payments were taking longer and longer. "Listen carefully," I warned him. "You see these doors?" I pointed to the front of the plant. "If you don't send me the skim milk, I'll have to close them, and you'll never get paid!" That got his attention. "Make up notes and I'll pay you," I said.

We made up notes for two seasons and continued to receive deliveries. In the meantime, as the one who managed the bills, I realized that Harvey was adding a surcharge. I was quick to let him know I was nobody's fool. "I know you're charging me 25¢ extra on each can, and when those notes are paid off, I want every quarter back!" I told him.

Two years later, Harvey's bookkeeper called to tell me that the last note was still due and that they had not received the check. I told him to have Harvey call me. But Harvey didn't call, he showed up at the plant instead.

"What happened to my last check?" he wanted to know.

"That covered all the extra quarters we paid per can through the years," I told him.

When Harvey heard that he carried on like a lunatic. Eventually Sam Miller himself had to show up to tell him to cool down, literally.

After that, we bought all our skim milk in tanks.

Reuben and I had a hundred ideas—some worked, some flopped—but Reuben seized control of our future with both hands, liberating the potential of his rich imagination. We meshed well together as a creative working team. Although we had no idea where our efforts would take us, we were willing to take our chances and find out.

ℭHAPTER Four

*—After learning the tricks of the trade,
don't think you know the trade.*

Back in 1905 a fellow named Frank Epperson in Oakland, California, invented fruit-flavored ice frozen around a stick. At first he named them Epsicles, and later, Popsicles. In 1924 he was awarded a patent for his product, which was advertised as the original drink on a stick. In 1925 he licensed his product to Joe Lowe, who had a bakery wholesale business in New York. Because Lowe was not in the frozen-food business, he licensed the product out to ice cream manufacturers, like Senator. We agreed to follow his recipes, buy the molds and ingredients from him, and use his packaging.

In the early 1930s Joe introduced the Twin Popsicle, which retailed for 2¢ and could be broken in two to share with a friend. In 1938 he introduced the Creamsicle, which was orange sherbet and vanilla ice cream mixed together and frozen on a stick. Somewhere along the line, he also created the Fudgsicle, a chocolate ice concoction.

Senator was the exclusive licensee for these products in the Bronx, and they were an enormous success, especially since the Joe Lowe Company did a tremendous amount of advertising. Popeye—the sailor of spinach fame—had a radio program at the time that was sponsored by Creamsicles. And if kids collected enough Popsicle, Fudgsicle and Creamsicle sticks or wrappers, they were eligible to choose from a number of prizes from the various Joe Lowe catalogs. In 1939, Lowe used the premiere of a Buck Rogers movie to promote his products, which was wonderful for us, because we made an increasing number of novelties for him. Lowe even invented a character called Popsicle Pete, who later became a hero in his own comic strip.

Senator became known as a novelty house. Reuben learned a lot about marketing from Joe Lowe, including the importance of licensing.

I remember that both times as I was nearing my due date I worked until the absolute last moment. I also remember what it was like when Reuben drove me to Bronx Hospital. Half our brains were focused on the business, and the other half on the coming baby. Natalie weighed ten pounds and took hours to deliver and Doris didn't weigh much less. A week after Natalie was born, my father died suddenly. No one told me and no one came to visit me at the hospital, so I didn't find out till later. I felt I had lost one of my best friends, and I never had the chance to say good-bye.

In the meantime, World War II raged around us. Reuben and I were like devils possessed, raising funds and knocking on doors, doing all we could for those who were in Europe, and then later, for those who were able to survive. Although Reuben was of prime military age at the time, he was also his mother's only son and sole source of support, as well as a married man with two infant daughters, so he was not drafted. My brothers did go to fight. Al became a decorated GI for his actions at the Battle of the Bulge and five other major campaigns. Eddie played the saxophone and was fortunate to become a member of the army band in Sicily. Jack fought in the Solomon Islands in Saipan, and came back with malaria that would eventually shorten his life. Bobby wasn't accepted because he had lost an eye in his childhood. My mother was proud that three of her sons were able to serve; America was the best country in the world.

Soon after Natalie was born, I was back at my desk. At the time we were living in a four-room first floor apartment. A typical day would start with Reuben leaving for work early and sometimes not making it back home. I would follow after I fed the kids and got them off to school.

Just around the time World War II broke out, Reuben met a man who really knew the ice cream business and knew how to produce a quality product. His name was Simon Levowitz. A brilliant technician, in the 1920s Levowitz had co-owned Renee's Ice Cream (named after his partner's daughter) in Newark, New Jersey. In the early '30s they had a falling out and Levowitz went to Denmark to work with the incredibly talented Danish-American inventor and entrepreneur John M. Larsen.

Years earlier, the Denmark-born Larsen had immigrated to Chicago and had been in the ices and ice cream business. He went back to his native country to develop his company, which eventually became Premier Is, a top-notch European ice cream manufacturer. The mechanically inclined Larsen used only the most modern machines for manufacturing, packing and distributing his ice cream product.

Levowitz helped design a plant built by Larsen that was near Copenhagen, and finished the job in 1938—just as Hitler was asserting his power. As a result, Levowitz returned to New York and found work as a general manager for Rose Associates, a real estate concern. When his wife became seriously ill, he desperately needed extra money for her care, and so he began to moonlight as a consultant to the ice cream industry. That's when he met Reuben.

During the war, we had lots of trouble getting sugar and other ingredients. Because of rationing, we had to supply records to the government of the amount of ingredients we used in our business. Although Senator had been in business for twenty years, Lea's methods were now backfiring. We had no production records and there was nothing accurate enough to prove to the government what supplies we needed. Levowitz was instrumental in establishing the criteria for us during the war and after in the post-war period.

We were lucky to have met him, and eventually he became Reuben's mentor. I admit it was hard to listen to Levowitz talk—he would drone on and on. But, on the other hand, he knew everything there was to know about making quality ice cream, and he had a profoundly forward-looking attitude that deeply influenced Reuben's thinking. After their long sessions, Reuben would come back bone-tired and say, "I'm exhausted, but from his mouth the pearls pour."

Levowitz taught my husband how to organize the production floor and control the business efficiently. His tutelage, combined with Reuben's voracious reading and experimentation, were the basis of our future innovations. Soon the improvements in our products and our hard work were visible on the books—although the postwar boom certainly had something to do with our modest success.

As the demand for ice cream increased, we needed to squeeze as much production out of the Southern Boulevard plant as we could. Reuben mastered the art of space-saving design and efficiency by turning production around in two work shifts and one cleaning shift. He even learned how to make the machines run faster and taught the workers to keep up with them.

When he would install a new machine, he would staff it with whoever was on the floor, and give them plenty of time to get used to it. As they gained confidence, he'd move a few workers back to the other machines. Then he'd ask the people at the new machines if they needed help, and they'd invariably say no, they were managing.

Levowitz also helped Reuben recruit younger people for Senator, including his own son-in-law, bright, ambitious 30-year-old Milton Hurwitz.

The postwar boom was a boon to us, but more so to big business. Not long after the war was over, big dairy companies began to take over the industry. As freezers came into common use, supermarkets took over as the most important outlet for ice cream, which was now being packed in bulk for family use. In the late 1940s, Breyers, Sealtest, Reed's, Horton's and Borden's were only a few of the huge operations beginning to offer supermarkets cheap ice cream—a pint for as little as 29¢, and half-gallons as "loss leaders" for 39¢.

Of course, this competitive pricing did not help our bottom line. But God seemed to always watch over Reuben and I and that Christmas, this Jewess received a God-given Christmas present. On my way home from work early one afternoon a week before Christmas, as I walked up the narrow, slushy street, I passed a few 8-year-old kids licking big green-and-red candy canes on their way home from school. They paused to let me go by.

"Hi!" I said, raising my eyebrows and pointing at the candy cane the middle one, a girl with shiny hair parted in the middle and bright green earmuffs, was holding. "That candy looks delicious."

A smile broke across her face. "You bet!"

"And I bet you like it, too."

"Yeah!"

"And who gave it to you?" I asked.

"*They* gave it to us!" said the little redheaded boy on her right, whose glasses were practically as big as his face. "The school gave it to us."

They started walking again, happily licking away. As I watched them disappear around the corner, my brain went into gear.

That night at dinner, I asked Reuben if he knew the

schools gave out candy to the kids for the holidays. He looked up from the book he was reading. "No. Nice of them. Kids must be happy."

"They sure are. I ran into a trio of them this afternoon. Do you think we could sell ice cream that way?"

He gave me a big grin. "Why, you bet we could! You just bet we could! Rosie, you are my secret weapon!" he said happily.

I'm glad he thought of me as his "secret weapon," because for the rest of our lives we gave each other all the help and love we could.

We started by going to all the local schools around the factory and talking to the teachers. "Why don't you come down to the factory and we'll give you Dixie Cups at the wholesale price," I told them. That would save them real money over the retail price in the supermarket. Dixie Cups filled with vanilla and chocolate ice cream were made everywhere, but with this initiative we could corner a large market.

In no time, teachers from all the schools in the area came to buy the chocolate-and-vanilla cups, packed 24 in a box. Our competition had no idea what we were doing.

I then launched phase two of my project. I went down to the Municipal Building in Manhattan, where they kept track of all kinds of information about the city. It was like a library. I found a listing there for "Board of Education," went in and asked the woman at the desk busy with some paperwork, "Excuse me, could you tell me what's in this section? I see it says 'Schools.'"

She had a very thin face with sharp blue eyes and her gray hair was pulled back in a severe bun, but she smiled warmly, put down her pen, and explained, "Well, we have the names of all the schools from every borough here, the names of the people who work there, the principal, teachers, the engineers, what salary they draw, their phone numbers in each school, and their home addresses." She pointed to where I would find Bronx information, asked me to let her know if I ran into any problems, and returned to her work.

I found the correct ledger and confirmed that it had a page for each school in the borough, as well as a good index.

I followed up immediately by sending circulars to every school in the Bronx, offering special rates for 20 dozen, for 50 dozen—the more you ordered, the less it cost you. It was Dixie Cup heaven. Soon, there were crowds of teachers in front of the plant, and people on the street were asking, "What the hell's going on there?" We were so busy it was like the tie store on the Grand Concourse all over again.

I told Reuben he had better hire some more people to do deliveries to the schools. Anyone with a car could make extra cash. It was cold and snowing, but our "summer-only" business was booming.

We used anything on wheels to deliver the stuff. We stayed up all night making sure everything was packed right in dry ice and set up for delivery classroom by classroom. We took in thousands and thousands of dollars that way, and it helped us make the bonuses and Christmas party that year.

We eventually spread the school ice cream business over the whole city of New York and made good money at it. I kept going down to the Municipal Building and spent entire days hunting for information. It was a win-win-win proposition; everyone involved did well. The teachers saved money, the kids had delicious ice cream, everyone who delivered made money, and our workers did well, too. Oh, yes, Reuben and I made a profit as well.

We did our best to compete with the ice cream behemoths and keep our heads above water. When the war ended, we created our own half-gallon loss leader—a product called Harmony Ice Cream—and sold it to Royal Farms, a chain of 30-something stores in Brooklyn owned by Charley Schreiber. They had a store in the Bronx, too. Because the demand was so great, we ran the plant day and night making enough Harmony to keep Royal supplied. But we were losing money on it, because we were undercutting our own costs. Harold Tarr, one of our salesmen, got a commission on every container we sold Royal. He was making good money and we were losing our shirts.

I tried to tell Reuben for months that we were selling Harmony too cheap, we weren't getting paid on time, and to top it all off, Schreiber was taking $400 off every single invoice for cabinet rental. When the cabinets broke down and all the frozen food products were ruined, Schreiber would force all the manufacturers to take their products back. To add insult to injury, we were paying Victor "Sonny" Maldonado, our repair whiz and a wonderful operator, to fix Charley's machines. We were hemorrhaging money. By the end of 1951 the Royal Farms account had run us $60,000 in the red.

One windy March morning in 1952, I stared gloomily at the general ledger on my desk, littered with memos and order sheets with hardly an inch of unused space. I had gotten out of bed that morning in a daze. I dressed, fed Reuben and the girls, and then sent the kids off to school. Reuben and I didn't say anything as we headed to work, coasting down the familiar streets to Southern Boulevard. I liked the quiet, and he appreciated the chance to let his mind wander. But I was worried. Normally I preferred to keep business out of our lives at home, and that included our time together in the car. But that morning I couldn't control myself. "Rufky," I finally said. "What are we going to do about Royal?"

We missed the light, and his fingers began to tap on the steering wheel. He began nibbling absently on his upper lip and the bottom of his mustache. "I don't know yet, Rosie. I'm still thinking about it."

I wasn't sure "thinking" was exactly the word for what he had been doing for months. We were in the worst situation we had ever faced in our business, and it wasn't getting better. Ten minutes later, we pulled up in front of the plant. I went to the office; Reuben went to the floor.

I looked up from the ledger at the neatly handwritten

list of bills pinned to the bulletin board. Planning to pay them in a few days, as I looked over the list I wondered if there were any bills I could hold back.

Then the phone rang. I picked it up and said, "Good morning, Senator Ice Cream," only to find the egg man's bookkeeper on the other end. Minnie Altschuler was going to whine about my account until I gave in. She could squeeze blood from a stone and was much better at getting money out of me than the ones who yelled could. I braced myself. "Yes, Minnie. What can I do for you today?" I was so polite I nearly choked.

"Mrs. Mattus, I'm so sorry to bother you like this, but you know. Well, the December invoices—for the powdered eggs, you know—are still outstanding, and I was just wondering if you could send us a check?"

I was looking out the window at the wind shadowboxing with an adolescent sycamore tree. A little push, and then another, and another, and then a sudden violent gust shoved it a foot to the side and would have knocked off all the leaves if there'd been any left. I said, "I understand, Minnie," feeling like the sycamore in the wind.

"Mr. Schwartz tries to be patient with you, Mrs. Mattus, but we're all struggling these days."

I closed my eyes and shook my head. "Yes, Minnie, I know. You tell Mr. Schwartz that I'll do what I can."

"Thank you, Mrs. Mattus. You know I wouldn't call like this, you being such an old account and all, but it's been rough on us lately."

"Of course, Minnie."

"We certainly appreciate it, Mrs. Mattus."

She hung up, and I added the egg man's name to the penciled list.

I was running out of options. I'd always been adept at juggling the monthly payments to the suppliers. They knew we were good for the money, and many of them, like old Joe Schwartz, had been doing business with us for 30 years or more, since the seasonal days when everyone carried everybody else through the slow times.

This was different. We were in real trouble, fighting a war against the giants of the industry, corporations with bottomless pockets. And they were winning, slowly, inexorably shoving us up against a locked door. Our deal with Royal was killing us, although it did provide some cash flow from week to week, enough to keep our people working and hold our suppliers at bay. But the pressure of trying to come up with money was finally getting the better of us. We were running the plant 24 hours a day—two work shifts to make Senator and the additional Harmony product, and a third shift to clean the machinery.

I started stretching out payments on due bills from 60 to 90 days and more, as a matter of routine, paying out a little at a time, and borrowing from the bank to make the payroll. We were robbing Peter to pay Paul—a lousy recipe for success—sort of like eating soup with a fork: You keep busy but you stay hungry.

There were 11 names on the list that morning; the previous month, there'd only been nine. I felt awful about it, but I couldn't see how I'd be able to keep juggling the bills without altering costs. So I put on a brave face and walked into the plant to find Reuben. He was working a machine out on the production floor, and I could see from a distance that he was still seething.

"Rufky," I yelled. When he turned, I waved to him. He came over and I led him to a quiet corner. "We really have to do something," I started.

He banged a fist into the wall, grinding his teeth so hard I thought I would have to add the dentist to the list. I thought he was going to have a stroke.

"I can't run a plant like this!" he ranted in frustration, turning his dark eyes to me. "Where's Harold? Did he come in yet? You let me know when he gets here! He's the only one who's making a dime out of this arrangement. I want to get rid of Royal, you hear me? Big customer. Big deal. His refrigeration's always breaking down; my mechanic runs out there all the time; costs me a fortune; we have to eat all the spoilages...and for what?" Then he calmed down and apologized to me. He knew when he'd pushed too far.

He never showed that anger more than he did on that windy morning in the Bronx. He came back to the office with me. Looking over the balance sheet I shoved under his nose, Reuben admitted, "You're right. This isn't working at all. Schreiber's doing very well with us. He's got a growing business, but we're starving to death here."

He held up a hand. Suddenly, something clicked in his brain. His whole demeanor changed. His eyes grew calm and confident as they always did when he knew where he was going, and a fighter's grin crept across his face.

"No! No, Rose! Those big guys, they're not going to do this to us. We're not quitters, and we never will be. Don't you worry. We'll find a way to make a living. And I am going to figure out a way to make them budge."

A few minutes later, when Harold strolled into the plant, Reuben was ready for him. When Harold heard that Reuben didn't want the Royal Farms account anymore, he became agitated.

"What do you want me to do?" he asked. "I tell him you don't want to do business this way, and he'll say, 'Fine, so long,' and find somebody else to give him the product."

"I don't care!" shouted Reuben. "I'll find another way. I do not want this business anymore."

"Look," said Harold, in a desperate attempt to save his account. "If you really feel that way, come to Brooklyn with me and talk to him."

Reuben crossed his arms across his chest in defiance, showing his distaste for confrontation. "No, no, no. I am 100% not going to Brooklyn with you. Take Rosie."

"Me?" I practically squeaked, I was so shocked. "Why are you sending me there?"

"You're definitely going to lose the account then," Harold warned him. "What's the matter with you? Schreiber's a woman-hater!"

Schreiber was maybe 15 years older than Reuben and had been divorced by his first wife. After that, he traveled regularly to Poland to pick up housekeepers who eventually became his mistresses. He was a thin, balding fellow, but he had a certain charm, dressed beautifully, and was very intelligent. I guess he was a typical CEO.

"What do you want me to do?" I asked Reuben.

"Lose the account," he said firmly.

"But what are we going to do with all the paper goods?" I asked.

We had already bought all the paper square half-gallon containers with "Harmony" logos. What would we do with all of it if we gave up the account?

Before I went to see Schreiber in his offices on Flatbush Avenue, I did my research and came up with details on every single one of his stores. I noted every time there had been a breakdown, every time Sonny had gone out for repairs. I prepared statements and put all the information into folders.

Reuben was convinced we needed another 3¢ on the gallon from Schreiber in order to break into the black. "Otherwise, you can tell him to forget about it, and come back to the Bronx. You handle it. I don't care what you do," he told me.

When I made my appointment with Schreiber, Reuben thought I would be telling the little king that we could not do business with him anymore. But I had something else in mind. Before Harold and I left for Brooklyn, I undertook another sort of preparation. I put on my best outfit and used my best perfume. I knew I could use my brains and my looks, if I had to, to get what Reuben and I wanted. Harold, in the meantime, was carrying on: "We're going to lose the account! He's going to throw you out! He can't stand women, and he's a very abrupt, impatient guy."

I had figured out a long time ago that men had big egos that needed to be fed. I knew, especially in those days, that a man liked to talk to a pretty woman who smelled nice. It may be politically incorrect to do things like that in business today, but don't fool yourselves, it happens every day of the week, and that's because it works!

The more Harold talked about Schreiber, the more I started thinking about ways to handle him. "Listen," I told Harold, "if it doesn't work out, it doesn't work out. We'll get other business. We'll be less busy, but maybe we'll make some money."

Schreiber's office was all the way out near Avenue X in Brooklyn. It was beautiful, with wood-paneled walls and matching furniture, the exact opposite of the environment Reuben and I worked in. He sat behind a huge desk, with light pouring in from the window behind him. It was open, and you could smell spring on the breeze that drifted in.

When we were ushered into the presence of the king of Royal Farms, Harold was right behind me. Schreiber fixed him with his cold blue eyes and said, "You. Out." As he closed the door behind him, he asked me to sit down.

"Are you Mrs. Mattus?" he asked flatly.

"Yes."

"Where's Mr. Mattus?"

"He's in the plant."

"So what do you do in the business?"

"I'm his little helper. I take care of all the money that comes in and all the money that goes out."

"Well, I certainly expected the owner to be here."

"He's busy," I said. I asked him to clear a little space for me on his desk, and put down my documents. "You know, Mr. Schreiber," I started, "I've heard a lot about you." I knew I was going to make him feel that I was not there so much for our benefit as for his.

He leaned back in his chair with his hands folded over his stomach. "You have? Like what?"

"That you're a tough businessman, which is good, but also that you're a *mensch* (a person of character). You do a lot of charity work."

His face, which was so hard you could strike a match on it, softened slightly.

"I came here to make you aware of certain things that are happening in your business," I said. "See, we like customers who make money, because if they make money, I don't have to worry—I know I'll get paid."

"Oh," he said sarcastically, "Is that right? What do you want to tell me?"

I opened my manila folders and showed him the records for each store—how much business each did, how much spoilage there was. I took out the folder for his largest store, on Junius Street, in a run-down area.

I started by discussing his new remote control unit, a device built into the ceiling that controlled all the freezer equipment in the store. "Let's take the store you do the most business out of, okay? You just bought a remote control unit, but there's something wrong with that equipment, because my mechanic is there all the time. Not only do you have spoilages in ice cream, you have spoilages with all your frozen foods. You can't be making money."

I went through every single store and showed him what the trouble was everywhere.

"I have a refrigeration department," he said, and picked up the phone. "Send in Pete," he barked into it. "I got Mrs. Mattus here, and she's telling me we got problems I don't know about."

"You're doing business with Ideal Fixtures," I went on. "Obviously they're not doing the right thing for you. You have to know about it."

Pete—a dark, heavyset Italian—walked in and Schreiber introduced us. "She's brought me a report about refrigeration problems in the stores, particularly the Junius Street location, the one with the remote units on the roof."

"Yes," Pete agreed, "we do have trouble."

"I have my man down there all the time," I continued.

"That's true," said Pete. "I know Sonny very well. He's a good mechanic. Sonny's around a lot; helps me quite a bit."

"Why should my man have to be there?" I asked. "Why doesn't Ideal, a huge company which you're paying good money to, take care of you?" Warming to the subject, I shifted around on my seat. "And it's not just me. What about all the frozen food in your cabinets? And what about the time you lose when the freezers are down? To say nothing of how I have to pick up the ice cream and throw it out! How much profit do we wind up with? How much profit do you lose?"

"Well," said Schreiber, "maybe you have a point there."

"I don't think, Mr. Schreiber, that my man should be coming here all the time. And why should I have to pay $400 on every check and take back spoilages?"

He cleared his throat, leaned forward, and began to tap a pencil on his blotter. "What else?"

"Well, I'd like to get paid a little faster. I don't even get my money in 30 days."

"You don't?" he sounded surprised, and picked up the phone. When he had the bookkeeper on the line he barked, "Mildred, see to it that these Harmony Ice Cream people get paid on time from now on...What?...Yes, you heard me right. And don't take off the $400 a month on the bills, leave them the way they are."

"And," I said, "Mr. Schreiber..."

"Call me Charley."

"No! I have respect for you. You're the head of the company."

"Call me Charley."

I took a deep breath. "I need another 12¢ on the gallon, Charley. I really do. You're a butter man. You know everything's going up—cream, butter."

He stared at me through his blue, machinegunner eyes, and for a long moment it got pretty quiet. Finally, he said, "Let's split it, okay?" Reuben wanted 3¢ more on the half gallon, I had gotten him 6¢.

Our deal was the basis of a lasting friendship. A few minutes later he asked me if I would be willing to work with him on some of his charity affairs. Of course I said yes.

We sat together in his office for almost three hours. When we finished going over all the papers and numbers and he was escorting me out, he said, "You know, your husband is a very lucky man." As he opened the door, he put his arm around my shoulder and sniffed appreciatively. "What perfume are you wearing?" he asked.

Harold was sitting there with his mouth wide open. Once we were back in the car, he couldn't shut up. As we made our way back down Flatbush Avenue, he kept exclaiming, "I don't know what you did in there!"

"What did I do in there? What do you think I was doing?" I said. "I showed him what was going on in his business, that's all, and asked for what was fair. Fair is fair."

When Reuben heard what I'd accomplished, he hugged me and grinned. "Rose, my secret weapon, for always."

Sometime later, Charley's secretary called and invited us to lunch with him. "Listen," he said when we got there, "I just got a proposition from Sunnydale Ice Cream. They want to give me $25,000 to bring in their brand. What do you think I ought to do?"

I said, "Well, you know, Charley, I really appreciate you telling us about this. We have the paper goods and we're set up for production for you, but we can't possibly give you $25,000. We can't match that. Those are big operators."

He nodded. "But what should I do?"

"Well, you have to do what's good for you. But that $25,000 has to come from somewhere."

Schreiber said afterward that Reuben swore he'd jump out the window if we lost the account. That wasn't true, but I laughed when he said it. But we didn't ever lose the account. Royal Farms stayed with us until Charley's dying day.

But even with people like Charley on our side, the big companies continued to erode our business. They had enormous clout and it was punishing to compete with them. They could crush us anytime. It was, Reuben liked to say, like trying "to slug it out with the sluggers." This was not a healthy thing to do, because one solid punch to the chin could put you out of the game forever.

As time went on, it became increasingly clear to Reuben that our survival depended on somehow doing something different that they couldn't do and we could. But what?

ℭHAPTER Five

*—Anyone who is not confused
does not understand the situation.*

Reuben was always an idea man. He understood that the only way to beat the big boys at their own ice cream game was to make something different, something they either had not thought of or did not know how to do. Because our Harmony brand was no longer bleeding us, we had some extra profit, and Reuben put it to good use.

His desire to create a better product did nothing to lessen the old arguments he had with his mother. She still wanted to spend as little as possible, and had no patience for his grand ideas.

When things got really bad at work, Reuben would take off with Philip Levine, a "friend" who owned a gambling house in Riverdale, New York. He and Reuben would sample the nightlife that makes New York City the capital of the world. Levine was a real character, the kind of guy who installed a bubble light in his car so he could ride around the city chasing hookers with his flashing light. One night he and Reuben entered a Manhattan bar and discovered a lady singer entertaining the customers. Her name was Frances and she took an immediate liking to Reuben. After a night of carousing with Levine, Reuben came home, smelling of alcohol and somewhat disheveled. I warned him if he ever came home that way again I wouldn't let him into the house.

While I was home the next day, the telephone rang.

"Hello, who is it?"

"This is Frances," the voice at the other end responded. "Is Reuben there?"

I had heard about Frances and I was going to put a stop to her shenanigans real fast.

"Listen, lady. This is Mrs. Mattus," I told her, "and if you ever call here again I will come down there and rearrange your face. Do you understand me?"

She did, and never called again.

In the early 1950s, when the pressure from his mother became too great, Reuben left. For one solid, awful month, he took a job in Bridgeport, Connecticut, with Pickwick Ice Cream, one of the big companies. I stayed in the Bronx with the children and went to work every day at Senator with Lea.

Every day, Reuben called home and told me how much he missed me.

"So come home, Rufky," I pleaded. "You don't have to be so stubborn.

After a month, he did return, but he always spoke of his time in Connecticut as his "college days." As usual, Reuben took advantage of the time and learned as much as he could from every Pickwick department he managed to visit.

When he came home from Connecticut, we thought one of the lessons he had learned best was that he could not live without me and the children, but a few months later, we were separated again. This time, a combination of pressures took their toll on him physically. We thought he was going deaf, and the doctor we consulted said he needed surgery.

Surgery has never been a laughing matter, and I refused to allow that to be his first alternative.

"Go down to Florida and get some rest," I told him. But I couldn't go with him because the children were still in school, it was already spring, and business was picking up.

Once the decision was made for him to go, I acted quickly. We didn't even take the time to buy him suitable Miami clothes. I just drove him to the airport, and he got on the plane without so much as a suitcase. I figured I would wire him money to buy what he needed once he got there.

In Florida, Reuben checked into the Sans Souci Hotel, right on the beach, and promptly did something that, at first glance, seemed greatly out of character: He signed up for dancing lessons. Maybe he felt guilty enjoying the tropical sun while I sweated in the ice cream plant. I was the dancer in the family. I loved the rumba, the cha-cha, the mambo, anything with a Latin beat. Reuben found a great Latina dance teacher who taught him everything he needed to know in order to keep up with me on the dance floor.

After a week, Reuben came back to New York, trim, tanned, fit as a fiddle, and, if anything, handsomer than ever. His ear problem was completely forgotten. In addition to a wonderful lover, I had a terrific dance partner. What more could any woman want?

The following winter, my mother stayed with the children while Reuben and I joined Lea and Eleanor in Miami, their winter retreat. Every night, we went out dining and dancing. One of our favorite spots was Ciro's, the hottest Latin nightclub in Miami.

When we returned to New York, Reuben announced he had a new idea. Hold onto your pocketbook, Rose, I thought.

"A distinctive ice cream, something really top class," he enthused.

I remember how the sunlight washed across his face as he sat at the kitchen table. The girls weren't ready for school yet, and already I could anticipate the ride to work with knots in my stomach.

"Sounds great, Rufky," I said, wondering how much money "distinctive" was going to cost us. "Go for it."

A fter World War II, the perennial ice cream industry problem of how to keep things cold became easier. In the old days we used blocks of ice harvested during the winter and stored in insulated warehouses. In those days our plant received 50-pound ice blocks, which yielded eight pieces of ice. These we sold to peddlers, who usually came on Sundays before they went out to hawk their ice cream novelties.

Believe it or not, I was the best ice cutter anyone ever saw. I would raise the axe over my head and bring it down on the ice just so, and a perfect piece would split off. Angelo, one of the Italian peddlers who bought ice from us, always gave me flowers after I cut him a block of ice. Years later, when Reuben bought an ice-cutting machine, he never let me go anywhere near it. He worried it was too dangerous. But some of our old customers still called me to cut their ice because I did a better job than the machine.

The new refrigeration technology allowed food manufacturers and producers to build walk-in freezers, trucks with refrigerated holds, insulated ice cream trucks and refrigerated cases for grocery stores. In only a matter of years, the corner grocery store gave way to supermarkets with their vast banks of freezers and refrigerators. These "ice boxes" changed everything in the food industry, including the ice cream business. Now bulk ice cream could be sold to homemakers at retail prices.

Because we had had such a good time in Miami, Reuben decided to name his new innovative ice cream

"Ciro's." Although Ciro's was still a far cry from what would become Häagen-Dazs, it was the first step in the right direction. It was a very good product and it was important for many reasons.

Reuben made this ice cream from scratch—the first time he ever really made his own ice cream mix. He'd used everything he learned over the years in its manufacture. And he turned it into a French ice cream, which means he added a little egg yolk to the mix. French ice cream sounds fancier, and that little bit of yolk enriched the mix to a point where we could call Ciro's a premium brand. What Reuben wanted above all was for the eating experience to be a delight. And so it was—a good product that tasted better than anything else on the market.

Legally, ice cream can be 50% air. Ciro's was no different from any other product in that respect, but the extra egg yolk improved consistency and made the product richer. Ciro's cost more per unit to make and sell than other ice creams on the market then, but it tasted good and felt wonderful in your mouth. Big chunks of strawberries and bananas were added to batches of mix, producing truly delicious flavors that, for the first time, went way beyond cold and sweet. Ciro's was available in vanilla, chocolate, strawberry, coffee, walnut, cherry vanilla, butter pecan and banana. We had mixed-flavor containers as well.

Convenience stores and delis were only the tip of the marketing iceberg—they were our old reliables. But supermarkets were flourishing and opened the door to a whole new class of customer.

From the beginning, Reuben wanted Ciro's to stand out from the crowd of containers in supermarket freezer shelves. To help him, he hired a team of top salesmen who came up with many ideas. Some he kept, some he tossed, and many he improved upon. Using his team's expertise, Reuben quickly learned that packaging means almost as much as the product itself.

In the old days, bulk ice cream was sold in plain white

half-gallon containers with the company's logo, the name of the flavor, and other information printed on a label. Ciro's first appeared in one-pint containers that Reuben designed himself. He came up with a round, squat container that, when viewed from above—as people did when they looked down into the store freezer—seemed much larger than all the other pints. In addition to the perception that you were getting more for your money, Reuben fulfilled that perception. Borden's and Sealtest were selling pints for 49¢. Ciro's was priced at 30¢. You couldn't get a better bargain than that!

And it came in so many different flavors. Reuben used a range of contrasting colors—different colors for different flavors, with pictures of the fruits or ingredients on the front. The visual impact was tremendous. For the first time, ice cream customers simply had to decide what they were looking for—and reach for it.

As part of his marketing plan, Reuben introduced an even bigger (and naturally, even more expensive) innovation along with the ice cream: new freezer cases which we called "Happy Cabinets." We spent hundreds of thousands of 1950s dollars on these boxes to bring Ciro's to the public.

Reuben's next challenge was making customers hungry for Ciro's even before they walked into the market. He devised an extraordinary storefront display that he provided to merchants free of charge. A silkscreen printer produced advertising with Day-Glo colors on black backgrounds. As far as I know, it was the first time black light was used as a marketing tool. When bathed in the light, the Day-Glo Ciro's containers were startling, immediately attracting the customer's attention. If imitation is the sincerest form of flattery, we were admired to the hilt. It wasn't long before Borden's also began using Day-Glo.

Our first real success, Ciro's was everywhere. It was in all the best stores, such as Kollner's, a German supermarket chain that had beautiful outlets on Long Island—elegant, spotless, food establishments with crystal chandeliers in the ladies rooms.

But not all the ideas Reuben came up with were successful. Take for example the "Big-8," an assortment of eight half-pint packages made by the same machine we used to manufacture our half-pint "Big Shots." The "Big-8" packaging included an over-wrap and slips attached to show the flavors. The paper goods alone cost us plenty, as did the coupons Reuben gave away. We placed the item with Kresge's on Fifth Avenue, in the Mid-Island Shopping Plaza in Levittown, and elsewhere. They never took off, but Reuben was unfazed. He always said, you could make the best product in the world, but if you couldn't sell it, you'd be buried with it.

Though the novelties we produced were the mainstay of Senator, Ciro's soon became a principal part of our business. We managed to break into the regular grocery stores and the discount chains. We were the first to introduce ice cream into Korvette's, Modell's and other discount department stores. Other chains that came on board were Daitch-Shopwell, the Big Ben stores, and, in Brooklyn, Packer's Supermarkets, all of them adding locations through the years. In time, we turned our attention to New York City and the other chains. When we realized what a winner Ciro's was, we put freezers near checkout counters in the major stores, and the product moved even faster. The store managers were happy and so were we.

Not surprisingly, the big dairy companies took notice of our success and determined to eliminate it. The name of the game in the food industry is to get your product on the supermarket shelves and, as much as possible, eliminate the competition.

In 1958, one of our salesmen brought in a big account, a supermarket chain that decided to use our product instead of Meadow Gold, a division of Beatrice Foods. While it represented a tremendous coup, it was also going to be expensive. Reuben and I agonized over the huge expenditure—more than $200,000—that we were going to have to lay out for replacement freezers.

The chain that was interested in our product did not have its own freezers; the ones it was using were supplied by Meadow Gold. As soon as the chain stopped buying Meadow Gold, however, the company would yank its freezers and we would have to replace them in order to provide a place to showcase our product.

"We don't have that kind of money," I said flatly the minute he told me.

"So what?" he barked. "So we'll borrow it. Isn't that what banks are for?"

As usual, it was Reuben who was the idealist and I the economic realist. "Rufky, listen to me," I pleaded. "Do you realize how much of a load that'll be to carry every month? We won't be able to manage it."

He shook his head impatiently. "What are you talking about, Rosie? We'll make it up on the volume alone. This is an enormous deal."

Needless to say, he got his way, and I had to make another trip to the bank.

Then the roof fell in. Early one afternoon, about two weeks after we went into hock at the bank and replaced all the freezer units in the chain's flagship store, three flatbed trailer trucks showed up at our plant in the Bronx, each carrying a freezer unit and scores of our product. Meadow Gold had given the chain something they were calling an "advance rebate"—in essence, a bribe—and we were out. Literally.

It was a crushing blow, the worst we had ever been dealt, and the whole staff seemed immediately aware of it. Our workers ran to the windows to gape at the trucks holding our goods, and you could have heard a pin drop.

All eyes turned to Reuben, who stood on the loading dock for a while with his arms folded, staring at the trucks. His face bore no expression. Then he shook his head, gave everybody a broad grin, and told them to get back to work. He disappeared inside the office and did not come out for the rest of the afternoon. When I stuck my head in to check on him, I found him tapping the blotter with a pencil, so deep in thought it took him a minute to notice I was there. He didn't seem upset or nervous. He was hatching a plan.

"How are you?" I asked.

"I'm fine," he answered. "Do me a favor. Call your brother, Eddie. I have an idea I need to talk to him about as soon as possible."

My little blonde kid brother, Eddie, had finished law school by then, paying his tuition by working for us as a pasteurizer and truck driver. Years later, he jokingly called Reuben his "mentor and his tormentor."

Eddie also called him something else.

Reuben was always reluctant to sign agreements or to put anything in writing, because he felt a man's word was his bond. His attitude was that if he had to put something in writing, then you couldn't be trusted. No matter how he tried, Eddie could never convince him that the purpose of a written document was to prevent confusion. Invariably, after a deal had been struck, Eddie had to make notes of what was discussed at such meetings in order to remember the details.

Reuben once made a deal in front of Eddie, who at that instance wasn't acting as his lawyer but was just there to give him old-fashioned advice. Although Eddie wasn't at all enthused about the negotiations, Reuben felt the deal was a fair one. Ultimately, circumstances changed and the fellow showed up one day five years later and said that he wanted out—he wanted to be paid off. There were two other people in the room affiliated with Reuben at the time and they wanted to see his contract. He said that he didn't have a written contract, what he had was Reuben's word.

They called Eddie in and asked him if he remembered what had happened five years earlier. Eddie went over what he recalled—the man agreed that they had essentially the same recollection—and despite Reuben's right to send the guy packing, he honored his commitment and even paid the man interest!

To Eddie, Reuben's action was the definition of integrity and earned him the title "Mr. Integrity," the name Eddie called him for the rest of his life.

After earning his law degree, Eddie specialized in personal injury practice, interning for legendary attorney Harry Lipsig, the "King of Torts," who worked bi-coastally with the even more flamboyant Melvin Belli. Although Eddie was being paid, he often swore that just watching Lipsig at work would have been worth the price of tuition.

By the time Reuben called on Eddie for help with the Meadow Gold situation, my little brother, who had been working as Lipsig's trial prep person, had learned a lot about the practical side of law.

Reuben understood he was being steamrollered by a massive corporation that wanted a monopoly. He needed to know from Eddie if he had any legal recourse.

"What recourse?" Eddie asked. I had called him that afternoon from the office, and he dropped everything to come to us that evening. "To be considered antitrust behavior, we would have to prove their policy is having a 'significant impact on the public.' There's no way you can prove that, is there?"

"No," Reuben admitted.

"And they can send your freezers back to you once the chain dumps you for them? That's the protocol, isn't it? The account has to provide the units."

Reuben clenched his hand into a fist and pounded the desk until it shook. "I'm talking about the way we got dumped, Ed. I'm sitting here with machines that I'm paying a fortune on, and we're dead in the water."

Eddie thought a minute. "Well," he said, "there I can give you a 'maybe.' We can go into court and claim that Meadow Gold deliberately undermined us by offering people this 'advance rebate' thing."

"They sure did, Ed. Where I come from it's called offering a bribe, and that stinks." Reuben's face glowed.

"Yeah, well, where I come from, it's called 'tortuous interference,' and that's illegal," said Eddie. "We can ask for injunctive relief. Maybe the court will go for it, maybe not, but whichever way it goes, it's sure to cause a public relations stink."

Reuben agreed, and then he and Eddie conceived a history-making idea. Eddie drew up the papers that provided a contract between Senator and our merchant-customers, which allowed our customers to work toward owning their own freezer equipment. The more Senator products they sold, the more credit they received toward owning the freezer box. The arrangement meant it was to our customers' advantage to sell our products over our competitors. Of course, it was a given that we would have to match Meadow Gold's "advance rebate."

The plan called for Senator to lease the freezer units to our customers, taking the payments from the sales volume so that the merchants would never actually have to pay us anything. However, the storekeepers knew that if a competitor tried to come in, the store would have to pay us the balance of the lease. The freezer could not just be returned on a flatbed truck.

Our smaller, independent customers were intrigued by this arrangement. Once they owned their own freezer box, they could put in anybody's product. However, we knew it would take about ten years for them to pay off a freezer box, and we weren't worried about anything that far in the future.

While Eddie provided the legal angle, Reuben proposed most of the idea. Eddie was amazed at Reuben's ingenuity and at his ability to think under the gun. Years later, Eddie would talk about Reuben's "prickly courage."

Unfortunately, the big supermarkets had their own big freezers and didn't need ours. But we had a lot of independent merchant-customers and, to make room for more of our product—which gave them more credit toward their own equipment—the independents were happy to have us cart off our competitors' ice cream.

Paying full retail price, we bought up all our competitors' products that were taking up space in the independent stores, and then we trucked all that ice cream up to our huge walk-in freezer in the Bronx. The problem was we needed that space to store our own product. We had to get that bought-up competitors' product out of our plant in a hurry, even if it meant we had to sell it at a discount.

I remember the summer day when Reuben called me while I was working in the office. "What about the farmers markets?" he asked. These were open-air markets, usually held in Long Island, where people looked for bargains.

"What about them?" I said.

"Well, there're tons of people wandering around those places. We should truck the stuff in the hardening room out to the Island and try to unload it that way."

"'We,' Rufky?" I asked, thinking about the days I would stay in the car while he walked the sand in Brighton Beach selling ice cream.

"Well, actually, I thought you'd be great at it, honey! You can sell. You're a born salesperson. If anyone can get rid of that stuff, you can," he said.

And so I became Miss Rosie the Demonstrator, one of those people you see in the supermarkets dishing out samples to customers. Only I did it decades ago, when no one else was doing it. Nobody knew I was a part owner of the company that had paid to have the ice cream I was selling taken off the market. We put out all the competition's ice cream, and it moved like hotcakes because we sold it for 20¢ a half gallon, a real steal. As the stuff would start to melt, I would take any price, as long as I didn't have to *schlep* it back to the Bronx.

I was dressed in a white uniform with my then-black hair done up in a high bouffant, hustling ice cream like it was going out of style. One woman who came wandering by our rinky-dink setup wanted to make a party for her child. "Can you suggest a gift for my guests?" she asked me.

"Why don't you buy a container of ice cream for each of them? It'll cost you 20¢ a piece, and you'll look like a queen!"

"But how will I get that home? It's so hot out."

"I'll give you some straws," I assured her. We both started to laugh. "Look, what are you worrying about? You get home, you put it in the fridge."

She was already nodding and opening her pocketbook.

I sold the last container in the cabinet when a guy came by and I asked him, "You like coffee?"

"Yeah."

"Take it, and I'll give it to you for 15¢."

I even went to other dealers and asked them to help me sell. One guy, an antiques dealer, a big fat fellow with glasses, said, "Never have I seen a saleslady like you! How about you come work for me?"

One of our competitors also came by and asked me who I was. "You wanna work for us?"

"No," I told him. "I'm just a demonstrator."

I came home with an empty truck to a husband with a big smile on his face. "You know, honey, you could sell the Brooklyn Bridge," he said.

When we bought up the competition's ice cream from the independent storeowners, we had to return the freezers that belonged to the other ice cream companies. The independents didn't want any more of our competitors' ice cream—they wanted only ours—and so the freezers had to go back.

The competition didn't appreciate our efforts, of course, but we weren't doing anything illegal. We paid full price for their ice cream, and gave it away for pennies, just to get rid of it.

Some of the big boys wanted to know who the Italian from the Bronx was—they just assumed that the owner of a brand called Ciro's had to be an Italian. Only a few owners of big companies guessed it was a pair of Jewish immigrants.

Our experience with the giant dairy companies was no different from the stories many others could tell. That's why we banded together with other independent ice cream manufacturers—such as Silver Crown, Smith Brothers

Rosie the Demonstrator (on right)
with Ciro's Ice Cream.

and Big Bear—to form the Metropolitan Ice Cream Dealers Association. Our avowed purpose was to resist Borden's, National Dairy and other corporations who wanted to put us all out of business.

I will never forget the meeting when the president, Mel Ginsberg, decided to pick a fight with Reuben. My husband was understandably proud of the packaging he had designed for Ciro's, especially the colorful containers that let customers choose what they wanted from the freezer quickly and easily. Small wonder it was widely imitated. At the meeting, Reuben got up and said, "You guys have me to thank for this color identification."

The problem was, he did not say "identification." Just as, years earlier, Lea's "Sanitary" had come out "Senator," Reuben's "identification" came out "indentification."

"When are you going to learn to pronounce English words properly?" Ginsberg barked. "If you can't talk, have someone else speak for you."

Reuben looked up at the ceiling as if asking forgiveness for what he was about to do. "Is this your briefcase, Mr. Ginsberg?" he asked innocently.

"What? Yes, it is."

"Good. Here it is." Reuben picked the briefcase up and swung it down so hard it broke Ginsberg's nose.

Ginsberg brought charges against him, but then promptly dropped them.

Usually Reuben's displays of physical prowess were more benign. He and Sonny Maldonado often horsed around at the plant, challenging one another to accomplish feats of strength. Once, Sonny lifted a 250-pound vat of sugar syrup six inches off the ground. "Let's see you do it," he taunted Reuben.

Reuben motioned Sonny to follow him out to the street where he promptly laid his hands on the rear bumper of a car and calmly lifted it two feet off the ground. Sonny knew when to cry "uncle."

It was a lesson Meadow Gold learned, too. Eddie's threatened lawsuit made them realize they were headed for a public relations disaster if they continued with their dirty tactics towards us. They soon backed off, and we and Meadow Gold officials reached an agreement that allowed storekeepers to make up their own minds about who would service them.

In the Meadow Gold affair Reuben managed to dodge a potentially fatal bullet, and realized once and for all that that he couldn't go on fighting the big guys—his pockets weren't deep enough. Instead, flush with the success of Ciro's, he decided to compete with Louis Sherry and Schrafft's—premium ice creams for premium customers.

Until the problems with Meadow Gold, Reuben had been fairly idealistic. He liked to say that experience taught him you couldn't play in the big leagues and expect to win unless you matched the competition dollar for dollar. He realized that making a name for himself or his product wasn't enough. He had to figure out a way to remove himself from the arena—to prevent an assault by the megaliths, to find his own niche, and do it in a way that prevented them from attacking, simply because it wouldn't be worth their while.

𝔊HAPTER Six

—The key to leadership is not to give up on your beliefs.
Great leadership is to build consensus around conviction.

Ciro's was a success, and some men would have been satisfied with that, using the proceeds to enjoy the better things in life. And in certain respects, that's just what we did. Reuben and I had always been opera lovers. We loved the drama and the excitement, but most of all we loved the music. Reuben always bought the albums and we lined the walls of our living room with Caruso, Maria Callas, Joan Sutherland, Roberta Peters and, later, Placido Domingo.

We had a box at the old Metropolitan Opera House on 39th Street. We sat just behind Milton Cross, the radio host of the Saturday afternoon broadcasts. Every other Wednesday, Reuben and I went into Manhattan to enjoy the opera.

I reaped the rewards of Reuben's dancing lessons in Miami Beach. Although we were always busy with the

Dancing diva and her mate.

business, we loved to go dancing. In those days, when you went to the nightclubs, you dressed up. Reuben always loved it when I wore short dresses because he always admired my legs. I had, after all, won a leg contest at Junior High School 109—the school picked the graduating girls with the prettiest legs to stand behind a banner, so that only our legs were showing, and I was the winner.

My prize for winning the junior high school contest was a beautiful, life-size doll. I always loved dolls, and even after Reuben and I were married I collected them. Whenever one of our suppliers wanted to send us a gift, he usually sent a doll because everyone knew I loved them. I still have most of my dolls—including the one I won in the junior high school leg contest.

But our main passion was reserved for the ice cream business. Although sales from Ciro's were coming in nicely, Reuben still had the ambition to make a product so good it would remove us as a target for our competitors.

Reuben was in his mid-40s by 1957, at the peak of his powers. He was still so handsome it sometimes made me smile just to look at him. Now he was a mature businessman with nearly 30 years in the ice cream business, but we were still working around the clock.

By then Natalie was 14 and Doris, 12, and we had moved to Rego Park, Queens. Compared to the Bronx, the air seemed cleaner. Simon Levowitz, the mentor whose philosophy of purity, quality and the avoidance of artificial additives influenced Reuben, had been renting the apartment and sublet it to us when he moved into Manhattan.

We owed more than the apartment to Levowitz. Aside from guiding Senator Ice Cream through wartime rationing, he shared with us his ideas, which dovetailed naturally with Reuben's. But his encouragement and positive reinforcement were his greatest gifts to us.

When Reuben talked about Levowitz, he recognized how much the man knew about the ice cream business. In a sense, Levowitz was the father of the modern ice cream industry.

Natalie, Rose and Doris.

Reuben's single-minded ambition was to create a super-premium ice cream. There weren't too many premium brands on the market then. Schrafft's was one of the few, and they were selling pints for 59¢ each, which was considerably more than the regular brands. Borden's, for instance, churned out a 29¢-a-pint supermarket brand to meet the demand for lower-price ice cream. The chains thought that was all people wanted, a relatively low-price product made with lots of air—sweet and cold, Lea-style.

Ciro's French Ice Cream, as successful as it was, still fell short of Reuben's dreams. He remained an impatient, ferocious perfectionist, hunting for that extra something to give his product more value. Maybe his drive for perfection had something to do with his imperfect childhood. Perhaps it was because in the early days, Lea would put him down whenever he came up with an idea. Maybe he wanted to generate her approval. Who knows? But whatever it was that triggered Reuben's drive, he always believed in himself and trusted his instincts.

He was picky about everything. He dressed impeccably when he had money, though he rarely remembered to carry any around. We both valued cleanliness and a sense of order, and we wanted to pass that on to our children. Reuben placed great store in "bearing," which he took to mean how you carried yourself through life. It explains, for example, why he got it into his head to give the girls Sunday horseback-riding lessons in Central Park. He was a class act and wanted his kids to have some class, too.

Every day Reuben and I rode to the plant together. Lea still preferred to take the subway in from Brooklyn and rejected Reuben's offer of a drive. I worked the phones to make sure the kids were home after school was over. I made arrangements with Scott's Restaurant on Queens Boulevard so the kids would have dinner, and we paid the bills and gratuities at the end of the week.

We used to enjoy ourselves on vacations in Florida and on trips to industry conventions. We visited Tahoe, Las Vegas, Los Angeles, San Francisco, Chicago, Europe, the Caribbean, and especially Israel. We loved to travel together and really enjoyed whatever free time we had.

Since Reuben enjoyed the unexpected, and since he also lost hundreds of thousands of dollars in pursuing some of his ideas, he also profited—on more than one occasion—from discoveries that would have evaded less driven people. He used to say it took Thomas Edison 1,000 tries before he finally invented the lightbulb, and that's how he learned what wouldn't work!

For Reuben, making a perfect ice cream meant finding an effective means of tracking what was going on in the plant. As a confirmed believer in the scientific method, he didn't want to be forced into guesswork. As with any food product, the end results always needed to taste, look and feel the same as the previous batch. And in order to get the same exact flavor, consistency or appearance every time, Reuben needed to record everything that went into the mix and what happened during every step of the process.

Reuben went to all the ice cream conventions—he was the first one in and the last one out—and looked at all the most modern equipment. Afterward, he would do his own research. We made several trips to Europe to investigate how the machinery was being used, and, in between trips to the factories, we had a good time in Denmark, Sweden, Belgium, and even Germany. We weren't particularly happy about going to Germany so soon after the war, but that's where the equipment was, and Reuben wanted to see it. Actually, the Germans treated us very cordially. Well, why not? We were their customers.

By the mid-1950s, we had four Creamery Package Company continuous freezers in operation at the Bronx plant. These machines allowed Reuben to experiment with the techniques that eventually helped him to develop the ice cream of his dreams. By 1958 Reuben knew these machines backward and forward and how to squeeze more out of them by fiddling around with the various knobs and levers.

In those days, most ice cream weighed no more than 12 ounces a pint. Most of what was in that pint of ice cream was air, which weighed very little. Reuben's idea was to make a heavier product that would taste better because it had less air pumping it up.

The idea was tantalizing, but the challenge was daunting. Most ice cream was selling for 49¢ a half-gallon, and the stores were using it as a loss-leader. Reuben believed there were people who would pay extra for a densely packed, home-style ice cream that was bursting with flavor.

The way he saw it, the new product would come out at 75¢ a pint, not 79¢ and not 69¢, 75¢ a pint, because he hated that gimmicky "nine." He liked fives and zeros. He told me about his plans for the weight per pint—and the price—for the first time late one afternoon in the early fall of 1958 as I sat in our plant office, going over the payroll.

"Seventy-five cents a pint?" I said, shaking my head without looking up. "Well, what do I know? Anything you say, Rufky. Anything's got to be better than selling half-gallons for 49¢." I waved my hand at the books, invoices and purchase orders piled on my desk. It grew very quiet. I took a deep breath and counted to ten. "Just tell me one thing, though."

Sitting on the edge of my desk, in typical Reuben fashion, he wouldn't look me in the eye and began fiddling with the stapler, "What's that?"

"Well," I said, really trying to be delicate about it, "why would people in their right minds spend that kind of money on ice cream? I mean, would you spend 75¢ for a pint of ice cream?"

"Oh, no! Is that what you think I'm talking about? No, no. You don't get the idea." He had a gleam in his eye. "Not 'a pint of ice cream,' Rosie, we're talking about a pint of the best ice cream you ever tasted in your life—ever." He swept a hand around the room. "It's our way out of this mess we're in! We have to make the absolute best, a special product nobody will even try to fight us over. We'll be able to make a decent living without the headaches."

The product he was thinking about would contain a lot of sweet cream, at least as much as the 14% found in Schrafft's. They would use only the best vanilla, fresh milk, fresh cream, the best chocolate and the best coffee. Reuben's taste buds were the ultimate decision makers as to what went into his ice cream.

And so, the experimentation and research process began. Accidents happen all the time when machines run 16 hours a day and the other eight are spent cleaning them. In one particular instance, serendipity arrived with an accident.

One day, the plant was making Ciro's when the air injection pump died. Suddenly, one of the people on the floor shouted that there was a problem. Reuben came running out of the office and saw that the conveyor was stopped. There seemed to be something wrong with both the air hose and the compressor feeding the air through it.

Reuben was already waving to Frances DeGennaro, one of the women on the floor. "Listen, Fran," he said, "Sonny's out in Brooklyn someplace. Pack everything up and put the stuff in the freezer." Sonny, our engineer, was always out on the road.

It was only when things quieted down that Frances noticed they'd missed three or four pints. She showed them to Reuben, who was astonished to discover that they hadn't yet melted. It didn't seem possible. Ice cream melts at room temperature and it doesn't take long. This had never happened before. Reuben put them on a scale and the pints weighed more than they should have. Reuben took a spoonful of this dense mix and said it was the best ice cream he'd ever tasted.

He gave me some of the vanilla, my favorite flavor, to taste. It was simply amazing.

"Rufky, you've really got something," I told him. It was the best ice cream I'd ever tasted. I'd never had anything like it.

From that moment on, he concentrated every waking moment on developing the best-tasting ice cream in the world.

There were decisions to be made, not the least of them how much air would be allowed into the mix. Even prestige brands like Louis Sherry and Schrafft's were pumping in enough air to lower the weight of their pints to 12 ounces.

The technological challenge of eliminating more than half the air in a pint of machine-made ice cream was difficult indeed. Test batches failed to produce usable results—the ice cream came out too runny, or it turned into butter, or it lacked "mouth feel"—that is, it didn't taste or feel right when you popped a spoonful of it into your mouth.

Reuben worked for months on end and settled on a formula for the basic mix to produce three flavors: vanilla, chocolate and coffee. The earliest samples of this brand-new as yet unnamed ice cream were packed by hand in the plant.

Whatever happened and however it happened, Reuben was finally able to come up with the necessary ratio of time, temperature and pressure. In the process, he created an excellent, exclusive, enhanced ice cream. He knew in his gut that people would indeed pay 75¢ a pint for it. And he was ecstatic about finally coming up with the way to make the ice cream he had been dreaming about since Eddie the Irishman told him that Lea's ice cream was garbage.

No question, the new ice cream he had discovered was great, but we had to figure out how to make money with it, and we didn't have any delusions about what it would take to achieve some decent market penetration. Basically, we now had a product with incredible potential. Years later, the newspapers would portray Reuben as an overnight sensation, but that wasn't true. We worked long and hard for years to get consumers to understand our product. Once they did, they happily paid premium prices for the best ice cream in the world. And that is no exaggeration.

But I'm getting ahead of myself. Before Reuben and I could even think about mass production, we had to come up with a name for the product.

I've said it before, and I'll say it again. Reuben was the kind of fellow who took us all for a ride on an emotional roller coaster. Yet whatever the crisis or idea he was grappling with, one thing remained paramount through good times and bad: Reuben cared about quality. As far as he was concerned, the way the world perceived his ice cream would be the way the world perceived him. He wanted to make a product he could be proud to call his own.

It took a long time for the little boy who ate ice cream at Ellis Island to make his dreams come true. Now, with the new product, it was about to happen. All he had to do was come up with the name, the name that would roll off people's lips when they reached deeply into their pockets and paid 200% more for a simple frozen dessert.

Because no one could ever point to the exact moment or circumstance that led us to our secret formula, everyone wanted to be part of the story. "Success has a thousand fathers and failure is always a bastard," I told Reuben.

We knew we had a superb formula and a great package design, based on the flared pint containers Reuben had used for Ciro's, but for months Reuben tortured himself with the question: "What's in a name?"

All of the quality ice creams had quality, dream-like names. There was Louis Sherry, Jane Logan, Lady Borden, and Dolly Madison. Reuben wanted something different, a different sound and a different image to distinguish his product from the pack.

One afternoon, he was sitting at his desk, turning a pencil around in his hands, muttering about "it." "It has to be different, special, and it has to convey quality—everything hinges on it," he said half to himself.

I didn't have to ask him what "it" was. For weeks he had been worrying over the issue like a dog with a bone and had not been saying too much to anyone about anything else. Now he was thinking out loud, and he needed me to be his sounding board.

Since I had to say something, I folded my hands in my lap and said, "Oh?"

"I mean, who cares what my name is? You put 'Reuben' on the package, who's going to grab it? It's got to have a catchy name."

I nodded and kept looking at him, encouraging him to continue.

"I think maybe a Danish name," he said suddenly, just out of the blue.

"Why Danish?" I asked.

"Well, they're nice people, you know. Good people. They tried hard to save Jews during the war, ferried them to safety ahead of the Nazis."

He had a point. "That they did, and God bless them for it," I said.

"Exactly. God bless them. As far as the rest of the world goes, this country doesn't like that country, and that one doesn't like this one, but everyone likes the Danes."

Warming to his subject, he got up from the desk and began pacing. "I like their flag, too—it's red. It'll make a good logo. I could put Oslo on there, and Copenhagen. Nice, friendly places. And it's cold there, too, you know, plenty of snow and ice. Makes you think right away of ice cream." So we settled on somehow incorporating the Danish flag onto the package.

In the meantime, Reuben developed the flavors (vanilla, chocolate and coffee). After a trip we took to Knott's Berry Farm in Anaheim, California, he added boysenberry sorbet. The boysenberries sang to Reuben's taste buds, and he brought home a huge supply. Soon he was buried in berries and ice—and loving it. As usual, he never focused on the cost. "I'm not making any money at it yet," he admitted with relish, "but I'll soon figure it out."

But what would we call the product? The name kept eluding him. He felt for a long time that it was on the tip of his tongue, but he couldn't quite get it out. Bits and pieces of ideas flitted past him, just out of reach.

Never one to tackle just one job at a time, Reuben set out to work more carefully on the packaging which would help with the marketing. He had a rare gift. He could say in a few words what would take someone else volumes. And he knew about the power of graphics and how to make a package design that would sell.

Sheldon Klein, a packaging salesman, was working for the Lily-Tulip Paper Company when in the course of his rounds he stopped at a gourmet shop on Mamaroneck Avenue in White Plains, New York. The counter display carried Callard and Bowser's English Toffee and his eye was automatically drawn to the candy because of its packaging. It was a new and impressive wrinkle in food design. When his route took him back to the Bronx, he mentioned it to Reuben. "It really caught my attention," he told Reuben. "Gives the wrapper a really elegant look."

Reuben told him what he was planning. He also told him he needed good packaging for the as yet unnamed premium "Danish" ice cream.

"Ciro's," Klein remembers, "had already done a color-coded lid with an illustration and a gold-foil surround—a marketing approach that worked well."

My brother Bobby, who was in the printing business, added to the mix with an idea for a gold-and-black lace wallpaper design that added a rich, elegant look.

Reuben's original design for the pints of the new product featured the outline of the map of Northern Europe, with stars designating Oslo (Norway), Copenhagen (Denmark), Helsinki (Finland) and Stockholm (Sweden). The whole thing was enclosed in a framed oval. The names of these far-off cities sent abstract messages to the consumer, all of them positive and none of them really having anything at all to do with ice cream. They evoked a sense of the exotic, while still exuding friendliness and tradition. On the back of the container, Reuben printed: "We have recreated an Old-World formula."

While working on the name, Reuben kept a dictionary on his desk, one with geographical places that he could consult while seeking an inspiration.

One night, his mind wandered to other fine-quality products on the market, one of which, he said, was Duncan Hines cake mixes, which we liked very much. "I like their quality," he said, repeating the name, "Duncan Hines, Duncan Hines."

He took a pencil and wrote the name on a piece of paper. "Duncan Hines. Hines Duncan. How about Hines Duncan?" he said. Then he just wrote down the initials. "H.D., H.D. How does that become Danish?" He asked. He began to play with the letters. "Hines Duncan. Haigen Duncan—how about that? Haigen Duncan. Haigen Doozken. Haagen Dazs. Yes!"

He jumped up and gave me a big kiss. "And we'll put an umlaut there, on the first 'a,' make it even more Scandinavian. We'll call it Häagen-Dazs."

Reuben didn't learn until much later that there are no umlauts in Danish, but by then it didn't matter. The trademark bore an umlaut, and with an umlaut it remained.

And that's how Häagen-Dazs was born—a different kind of ice cream, one with only 20 percent air and 17 percent butterfat at a time when everyone else's ice cream was half air and the law required only 8 percent fat for flavored ice cream and 10 percent for vanilla.

&HAPTER Seven

—Vision without action serves no purpose. You can change the world if you have vision with action.

While Reuben was busy experimenting with ingredients and freezing points, I had to come up with the money to pay for his new ideas. Above all, we had to negotiate favorable seasonal contracts with our suppliers. We had, after all, committed ourselves to making the best ice cream money could buy.

Reuben was happier than I could remember. If he had been single-minded while conceiving his idea, he was like a tornado when we entered the development stage. We never quite knew what he was going to want next. Sometimes I think he didn't know either.

One afternoon, he shouted at everyone within hearing range, "Get me all the pots in the hall closet." Another time, he had another thought. "Go find every brand of vanilla extract you can in the supermarket," he barked.

As he and the tasters he hired settled on various formulas, we sent samples of each new flavor of Häagen-Dazs to a number of testing labs to verify their quality. Doris and Natalie, our brothers and sisters, nieces and nephews, were all given samples to confirm the taste results.

Our heavyweight product with the funny name came on the market with three flavors: chocolate, vanilla and coffee. It took Reuben six years to figure out how to make a strawberry that satisfied him.

As for rum raisin, which became so many people's favorite flavor, this was indeed a challenge to create. But for Reuben there were never problems, only solutions—and he found his. The 100-proof Jamaica rum was less expensive than some of the other top-quality ingredients we began using (such as macadamia nuts), but it was costlier than milk and sugar. First, Reuben had to find the best crop of raisins (and when a crop failed, don't ask about the problems we faced), and then he had to figure out a way to keep them tender and juicy once they were frozen. He solved the problem by first seeping the raisins in the alcoholic rum, thus lowering their freezing point.

The leading ice cream expert at the time was Wendell Arbuckle, a professor of dairy science at the University of Maryland. He had authored what was considered the bible of commercial ice cream production, and most of the big companies used him as a consultant. Reuben sent Professor Arbuckle a sample of Häagen-Dazs and asked him to evaluate the new product. Arbuckle must have thought we were nuts. "Too soggy and heavy," he told Reuben.

Arbuckle deemed Häagen-Dazs "defective," but instead of feeling dejected, Reuben was elated. If the industry maven thought the new product was so different from the standard that he thought it was a mistake, it meant to Reuben that he was getting closer to his goal.

I told him not to pay any attention to what Arbuckle said. "You know everything there is to know about the ice cream business," I told Reuben. "What do you care what any professor has to say?"

Reuben started to laugh just thinking about what I would have to say to the professor. When things were good and when things were bad, Reuben and I always had each other.

Even Lea, when she tasted the new product, stayed quiet.

Though Ciro's had been a very successful product, Häagen-Dazs was in a class by itself. By 1960 we knew Häagen-Dazs was more than just another ice cream, but we did not know how to sell it. We knew in our bones the new product was better than Ciro's and would help us accomplish what Ciro's never could—a safe and secure business, free from the problem of competitors whose products were never going to be as good as Häagen-Dazs.

Reuben decided the best way to start our Häagen-Dazs business was to retrace our steps, doing what we did at the very beginning: we had to give the ice cream away. So part of our sales strategy for Häagen-Dazs was to load up the car as we did in the old days, and drive around, handing out ice cream. Reuben firmly believed that giving out samples and relying on the subsequent word of mouth would be worth millions.

"Once people taste Häagen-Dazs, they'll come running back for more," he said. "We'll build brand loyalty."

"Even at those prices?" I thought to myself.

Neither Reuben nor I believed Häagen-Dazs would be an overnight sensation. I don't believe Reuben realized how long it would take for Häagen-Dazs to become a hit, nor am I entirely sure he particularly cared. He operated by instinct, by the seat of his pants. We knew what hard work meant, and we weren't afraid to put in 16-hour days, working towards a goal.

Reuben believed in slow, sure achievement earned by word of mouth, pressing the flesh and cumulative recognition. He had little faith in advertising, considering it a waste of money. He used the media sparingly, serving as his own public relations man. His outsize personality, photogenic style, smile, and great love for his product made him a poster boy for the great American success story. He was so sure of himself, he convinced me.

Our next challenge was to convince store owners to carry our expensive item. One of our answers was Larry Muney.

Larry Muney came into our lives in 1957. He'd been in the egg business, doing everything for an outfit in Pennsylvania, from candling and boxing to selling. His true vocation was that of salesman. He was a natural, one of the best people I ever met at cold calling—breaking new ground—when he'd show up out of the blue and push his product until he walked away with an order, any kind of order. His technique was direct and simple. He'd buy a map and start driving around in concentric circles, widening the circle as he went, looking for places that wanted to buy eggs or anything else he might carry. In the course of his travels, he hit every conceivable outlet.

One day, as he was driving down Southern Boulevard, following his formula, he found a place that looked like it made good potato salad and coleslaw. It was Gersten's, the landlord who shared half the building with us. By mistake, Muney walked through the wrong door—and there was Reuben, running the Vitaline machine that produced novelties. It was a fateful encounter, destined to change all our lives, including the Gerstens. Even Lea was there that day. I was busy in the office, and Larry was ripe enough for Reuben to pluck from the Pennsylvania egg farm.

"No," he told Muney with a grin when he found out what the tallish gent with the mustache wanted, "you're looking for the place next door." But they started talking anyhow, as is Larry's way, and Reuben was immediately impressed by his manner. "Look," he finally added, "we don't have potato salad and coleslaw, but we do have ice cream."

"Ice cream?" replied Muney, who sensed a kindred

spirit. "What the heck, that's okay. Coleslaw, ice cream—I go to the same markets."

Reuben nodded with enthusiasm. "Okay, then! Why don't you see if you can get me some business?"

Muney went out and, two weeks later, came back and handed Reuben a list of outlets he'd signed up, cheerily announcing, "Well, here you are. This is what I found."

"I'm getting calls from all over the place complaining about how you're stepping on other people's toes."

Muney shrugged—nobody had told him what was off-limits.

Reuben thought it was funny. "You have to be a little more careful where you go, but I really want to hire you."

They soon came to an arrangement and Muney started pushing Ciro's. And then Häagen-Dazs came into being. In his usual go-get-'em way, Muney drove the roads of New York and New Jersey, bringing Häagen-Dazs pints to anyone who would try them. He was nothing if not tenacious.

Every day, he would load up the back of a station wagon with 70 gallons of ice cream wrapped in moving van blankets and delivered them personally. Sometimes, especially during the winters, when it was too cold to keep the car windows open, the smell of dry ice would almost knock him out.

Larry helped build a network of outlets for us in the greater New York metropolitan area and, later, in California, in his patient, single-minded way. Store owners admitted they eventually caved in and put Häagen-Dazs in their freezers just to get rid of him. More than one supermarket manager and convenience store owner told him, "All right, all right. I'll put this stuff in, but don't let me see you around here again."

Slowly, Larry, Reuben and I developed markets for Häagen-Dazs in the supermarket chains. The first one we landed was A&P. Then came Grand Union, Waldbaum's, Daitch-Shopwell, Food Town and King Kullen in New Jersey. Later came King's and Gristede's.

Larry, and sometimes Reuben or I, always took along pints of Häagen-Dazs when we went to the stores. We would fill four or five rows in each freezer, and then turn ourselves into demonstrators, offering samples to customers as they shopped in the aisles. It was just like the old days at the flea markets when I had to sell the competitors' junk, but now we were selling our own superior product.

After spending time with the managers, we would put samples of Häagen-Dazs on doily-covered trays. Sometimes, we'd scoop samples out with a melon baller and serve the flavors on small, bland cookies. When that became too expensive, we switched to paper cups. We threw ice cream around, making shoppers feel as if they were attending a party rather than carrying out their daily chores.

When we weren't working the supermarket chains, we spent time developing the independent delicatessens and convenience stores. Unlike the supermarkets, these small businessmen, for the most part, didn't own the freezer units in their stores, since the mom-and-pop stores never generated enough volume to buy direct from the producer. Instead, they used jobbers, middlemen, who, for a percentage of the profit, provided the freezers and filled them. And so in Häagen-Dazs' early days, when we certainly couldn't afford to supply freezers to hundreds of convenience stores as we once had to Charley Schreiber, our success depended on our ability to use the other guy's freezer. We were peddling America's most technologically advanced ice cream the same way Reuben peddled Lea's "cold and sweet"—essentially from a horse and wagon. The jobbers for Louis Sherry and Schrafft's did not particularly appreciate finding Häagen-Dazs pints stuffed into the freezers they had provided for their products, but their complaints fell on deaf, Häagen-Dazs-happy ears. It didn't matter how far in the back of the freezer the jobbers stuffed our pints. The customers found our product because they wanted it. They often came into the deli or convenience store in the first place because they wanted to buy a pint or two of Häagen-Dazs.

We gave out samples of Häagen-Dazs in delis and convenience stores from 125th Street to South Ferry, covering most of the island of Manhattan, a veritable ocean of stores. We would leave them with a couple of gallons of ice cream, and when these sold like hotcakes, and consumers came back asking for more, the stores would turn into regular customers. We no longer had to find schemes to convince these store owners to carry our product, like we once did with Ciro's. Everyone wanted Häagen-Dazs.

Reuben happily supported the Häagen-Dazs sample giveaways, but I was always worrying that we were burning money. For Reuben, who saw only the fact that he was keeping the major companies at bay, the risk was worth it. Again he was right. People willingly paid premium prices for the best ice cream they'd ever tasted. It took three or four years to establish the core network, but it was accomplished without a dollar's worth of advertising.

With hundreds of flavors, brands and sizes vying for a relatively small amount of freezer space, our advantage was Häagen-Dazs' price—which generated a lot of profit for the amount of space the product took up. Once again Reuben's genius paid off.

Almost from the beginning, we found an alternative market, one steeped in the marijuana culture of the '60s. Uniquely appreciative of Häagen-Dazs and Häagen-Dazs alone, our early clients were a motley assortment of oddballs with long hair, fringe tastes and decidedly eccentric business styles. We thought that this avenue could never generate direct sales volume on a national or even a regional scale, but we were wrong. Their effect on the market was astonishing.

Building on a highly sophisticated, cosmopolitan interest among Manhattanites with expensive tastes and a capacity to set fashion trends, Häagen-Dazs became a celebrity in its own right. It became a symbol of luxury and indulgence in ways no white-bread sales campaign could have predicted—and that, ironically enough, led to phenomenal success beyond anyone's wildest dreams.

We first uncovered these possibilities in 1963, when Reuben attended a New York Coliseum trade show and met a fellow dressed in the style of the Pennsylvania Amish, except that he had no beard. He represented Faith Farms, a health food operation that took him all over the country. By then, we were making honey vanilla and carob, two 100% natural ice creams, and he wanted to carry Häagen-Dazs, especially after he learned that we abhorred artificial ingredients. For the next two or three years, his business delivered pints of Häagen-Dazs to small college towns across the country by Greyhound bus.

In the 1960s, the flower children also came on board, when we brought the product to David's Pot Belly on Christopher and Bleecker Streets in Greenwich Village. The eatery was owned by Bruce Waite, whose brother Ralph played the father on the TV show, *The Waltons*.

Bruce, who operated an organic foods restaurant, was serving goat's milk ice cream and it was awful. He fell in love with Häagen-Dazs and decided it would be his signature dessert. Since he was located on the most avant-garde corner in an avant-garde neighborhood, he brought eccentricity to his marketing campaigns and would run an annual "Miss Häagen-Dazs" contest—fat girls and skinny ones and bisexual ones and transsexuals, a phenomenal idea in those days. Bruce was sharp as a tack and nimble in his business life and in his understanding of the way the world worked. We stayed close to Bruce, and, years later, he credited Reuben with saving his and his family's life—because Reuben taught him something that had nothing to do with ice cream: "If you get into a place, make sure you know how to get out." Reuben never went into a hotel, restaurant or store unless he knew how he could get out in case of an emergency. In the 1980s, when the MGM Grand Hotel in Las Vegas collapsed, Bruce and his family escaped because he remembered what Reuben had told him.

Bruce was one of the first people to see the business opportunity in serving Häagen-Dazs by the scoopful. He loved Häagen-Dazs and Reuben, and so believed in the future of the product that he started to dip Häagen-Dazs right next door to the Pot Belly. People would pull up in taxicabs, jump out to buy a scoop for themselves and one for the driver, hop back in and speed off. That was a first in the Big Apple. No one had seen behavior like that before! Not for ice cream, anyway.

In 1970, Gary Furgeson, another entrepreneur, was the first to open a Häagen-Dazs "dipping" store on Second Avenue and 69th Street. He eventually moved up to 86th Street, between Second and Third Avenues.

These were young New Yorkers whose personal values and lifestyles were totally different from Reuben's and mine. But Reuben understood that these hippies' turn-on, drop-out culture was one of the true engines driving our product.

"I saw that everyone was young," he explained once to a business reporter. "These were people who had never really tasted a quality ice cream. They weren't born when hand-packed and hand-dipped ice cream was made. They'd grown up on the 50¢-a-half-gallon brands."

Häagen-Dazs was changing the way these young people viewed ice cream. As the product became increasingly available in college towns, the kids became avid customers. When they went home for the summer, they did not forget their favorite dessert.

"The kids would go home for the summer," Reuben said, "and start checking all their local grocery stores to find out which ones carried our ice cream. By the middle of the summer, we'd be getting phone calls from store managers all over the country. They wanted to know how they could get our pints into their stores."

To put it simply, Häagen-Dazs ice cream ranked as perhaps the best taste sensation to reach for when you had the "munchies," and the word spread quickly through the young communities on campus and in towns.

Then along came a fellow named Zach Glickman. Everybody called him "Fat Zach" for obvious reasons—he was small, swarthy, fat and on a perennial diet. A music manager, he had started out as a roadie for R&B groups and had graduated to managing acts like Dion and the Belmonts and Frank Zappa.

When he contacted Reuben in the 1960s, he had a problem. Born and bred New Yorkers, he and his wife Alice were two of our earliest fans, really crazy for Häagen-Dazs. Now they were in a panic. They had to relocate to the West Coast, where there was no way for them to indulge their Häagen-Dazs habit. So the two entrepreneurs made a deal, and Häagen-Dazs went west.

Glickman brokered a deal with Arden Farms, a large California dairy operation, to distribute the product and, down the road, when volume increased to the right level, they'd manufacture it for us as well. For his efforts, Zach would get 10¢ on every gallon of Häagen-Dazs that Arden sold, in perpetuity.

Selling Häagen-Dazs was the case of the better mousetrap all over again. People wrote from all over the country asking how they could get Häagen-Dazs into their area. Real fans even volunteered to distribute the product themselves—and in the absence of any real overall marketing strategy, that's how the distribution system grew.

I remember Alan Strom, a middle school teacher who had left New York for Denver. When Arden Farms notified us that they were going to drop Häagen-Dazs, Reuben and Kevin met Strom in Denver, rented an eight-by-ten-foot refrigerator container, and shipped him a mixed pallet (255 gallons) of ice cream. After school and on Saturdays, Strom sold our carob and honey vanilla products to health food stores. When he started making real money, Strom quit teaching and founded Ultimate Ice Cream.

Reuben and I tried to give our distributors as much support as possible, but, at the beginning, there wasn't too much we could do. We were all struggling, waiting to

Frank Zappa.

see what Häagen-Dazs was going to become. And so we worked with all sorts of distributors with all sorts of requirements and problems. Reuben understood them well because we knew what it meant to start a business from nothing but dreams.

As the business began to take off, Lea passed away. For years she had been living with Eleanor and her husband Eddie in Brooklyn, wintering with them in Florida. That September, while in Florida, she had a stroke.

I was talking to her on the phone. "How are you Mom?" I said. When she answered I noticed that her speech was slurred and irregular. I spoke to Eleanor and told her I felt there was something wrong. Eleanor told me they'd been out the other night and Lea had spilled coffee all over the table.

When Reuben got home I told him about my suspicions and we immediately decided to take a trip to Florida to see what was going on. When we got there, Lea was in the hospital. As she lay on what would be her deathbed, she finally let Eddie have it for all the years of mistreating Eleanor. *Du bist ah mudnah mensch* ["You're a strange man"] she told him as he stood at the foot of her bed.

Lea passed away on September 8, 1971. Her body was brought back to Brooklyn to the Joseph N. Gorlick Funeral Home and then buried at Mount Hebron Cemetery in Flushing. For me, it was a great loss. Though Lea had a forbidding personality, she had always been very good to me and we had had a wonderful relationship.

Eleanor was soon gone, too. A year after Lea's passing, my wonderful sister-in-law passed away as well. When I heard she was ill, I called to tell her I was coming to see her but she told me, "Rose, you work too hard. I don't want you to come down here. Take care of what you have to do." That's the kind of selfless person she was. I went anyway. By the time I got there, however, she was already in a coma. I spent 13 days by her side until she passed away on November 15, 1972. Her *mudnah* husband never came to see her the whole time I was there, too busy

Lea Mattes.

Rose Vesel Mattus

walking the streets telling people how sick his wife was
...and then finding a job with a competitor.

&HAPTER Eight

—Happiness is an achievement.

After graduating from Forest Hills High School in 1958, Doris spent five years working in the office, answering phones and also occasionally doing supermarket demonstrations. At 18, she married a man named Arnold Horowitz, who worked for us in the Southern Boulevard plant. When her first child, Caryn, was born in 1963, she stopped working.

Natalie, on the other hand, chose a completely different path. She is now an adjunct professor of education at Pace University, where she is teaching teachers to work with learning-disabled children.

When Natalie was born, we had no time or money and so her first months were spent sleeping in a dresser drawer instead of a cradle. We tried to be good parents, but the business consumed us, and Natalie became a loner. Through high school, because she was taller than most of the girls, she felt awkward and gawky and says that she didn't bloom until she fell in love and married Evan Salmore, a very decent and good man.

As a child, Natalie liked to do her own thing and go her own way. She decided not to go into the family business, choosing instead to get her bachelor's degree at New York University. She also attended Parsons School of Design, one of the most prestigious art schools in America.

Natalie hadn't planned on becoming a teacher, but a stint at *Glamour* magazine and another with a buying office convinced her that teaching was more her métier. As Evan worked his way through law school, Natalie went back and earned two master's degrees: one in education from City College and another from Manhattanville College in professional studies.

Natalie was now qualified to teach learning-disabled students and worked at it most of her married life. She took four years off to have her kids, Michael and Paul, and then went back to teaching because she missed it. Through the years, she taught people of all ages, from kindergarten to adult education to the postgraduate university level.

Teaching allowed Natalie to find herself. Working with young people who had emotional, social and learning problems was a challenge she relished and it made her evolve and develop a passion for teaching and love for students that she didn't know she had.

Natalie retired from the city school system in 1996, and in 2001 returned to teaching at the university level. She says it's her turn to train teachers and she enjoys every moment, often traveling across the country to attend conferences about cutting-edge programs to bring back to her own students. Michael is planning to follow in her footsteps as a teacher.

Doris' son Kenny was born in 1971, and soon after Doris went back to work, but not for us. She was the second woman McCormack Foods ever hired to sell their spices, joining them as a part-timer. She did very well, and a year later, at a grocers' convention in Atlantic City,

Natalie Mattus Salmore.

Doris Mattus Hurley.

she met the head of the company. He didn't know who she was or that her family had a business, but he was so taken with her that he offered her full-time work.

Reuben thought it was crazy for Doris to work for someone else full-time and said so. He topped their offer and gave her $15,000 a year, a decent salary in the early 1970s.

The 1970s was also the advent of the Kevin Hurley era. Kevin's involvement with Reuben and Häagen-Dazs was one of the principal forces influencing our destiny. He worked with us at different times, and is still involved in family business.

Tall and good-looking, Kevin the businessman was tough as shoe leather, and started in the ice cream industry immediately after graduating from Fordham University in 1962. He began as a salesman for Pickwick Foods, the Connecticut-based ice cream company Reuben had worked for years earlier, and set about learning the business.

In mid-1970, the owner passed away and left the company to his sister—who quickly ran it into the ground. After 12 years with them, it looked like Kevin had no future. He stuck it out, though, taking the company into bankruptcy protection and doing everything he could to straighten things out. His short-term goal was to sell the business, pay the bills, make the payroll and have something left over for the sister. Employees even suggested he head a group to buy the company, but he decided against it.

Eventually, Kevin succeeded in dividing the operation in half, selling the manufacturing division and the distribution network to respective companies (manufacturing to a manufacturer, distribution to a distributor). Milton Hurwitz, who had also worked there and left when the owner died, came to Reuben to take over production. He told us about Hurley.

By 1972, Häagen-Dazs was producing over 300,000 gallons a year and Reuben realized he needed help. He could no longer run production as well as sales and still hope to take the company national.

When Reuben said he was interested, Milton got in touch with Kevin and set up a meeting. After they met, Reuben offered him the position of national sales manager, which Kevin initially turned down. At that time, Mel Cole, a friend of his who had once worked with Kevin at Schrafft's, had moved up the ranks of Stouffer's and was now offering Kevin a job there. Stouffer's was more appealing to Kevin than Häagen-Dazs because it was a new venture with an already established multinational company.

While at Stouffer's, Kevin helped develop new products. Cole moved to Scarsdale to be close to the New York market, but because Stouffer's was based in Solon, Ohio, Cole was too far away to protect his division's interests within the company. When Stouffer's cut back on advertising and narrowed the division's marketing effort, Kevin saw the handwriting on the wall and made his way back to Häagen-Dazs in 1974. Reuben said he was glad the big guy had finally come to his senses, and appointed him national sales manager.

In 1974, we began to make an impression on the market. One health food distributor started coming in and picked up honey vanilla and carob, which he *schlepped* around the country two pallets at a time. We could feel the product taking on a life of its own—it wasn't overwhelming, but it was moving.

"This is nothing," Reuben used to say, "that's nothing, but a thousand nothings killed the wild boar." In many ways, he saw himself as a teacher, and he enjoyed bringing these novices into the business, showing them the ropes, watching as they absorbed his knowledge and turning it to their own success. It's lucky he did—during those years he had to build a national operation largely by teaching other people what he knew. He loved to expound on life, too, and to apply the lessons he learned to his business.

Between 1972 and 1980, many other people joined us, and the product's reputation grew bigger than the

The guys at the South Bronx plant.

product itself. It began to define people's tastes, their sense of exclusivity. The *New York Daily News* asked, "How can you tell a snob? They have Häagen-Dazs Rum Raisin in the freezer." *The Times* also came up with a story about the founding of the company: Reuben had "rediscovered the famous ice cream 100 years after its invention by Jan Häagen, a Danish merchant of Dutch descent... Recognizing its worth, Mr. Mattus, a friend of the Häagen family, initiated the first distribution of the gourmet product in the United States, where it became an overnight hit." It was a better yarn than the real one!

Moreover, Reuben started being invited to academic institutions, like Rutgers University, to deliver lectures to the student body. He became part of a program that invited business people into academia to teach students about the business world, and when Reuben was on the agenda there were standing-room-only crowds in attendance.

Kevin Hurley's earliest exposure to this clientele came at the trade shows and conventions. "Better than sex!" he was assured by people who seemed to think they knew for certain. A woman declared, with only a trace of humor in her voice, that her idea of heaven was "a bath in chocolate Häagen-Dazs." He was struck by the drug terminology that some fans used to describe their relationship to our elegant pints of ice cream. They were "hooked," they were "addicted," they "mainlined" the stuff. A "hard-core user" had suddenly emerged, someone who would skip the serving dish entirely and eat it right out of the carton. "I tell you," Kevin says to this day, "I'd been in the business for ten, almost 11 years by then, and I'd never, never, seen anything like it before."

Kevin, himself an ice cream junkie, had the best of all opportunities to indulge his passion. In the course of production, when Häagen-Dazs comes off the freezer at 20°F.—just a little colder than it does from a soft-serve machine—it tastes even better than it does when you buy it in the supermarket or at a dipping store. There was nothing like it. Kevin used to eat chocolate Häagen-Dazs at just that moment, right off the line—and in density, smoothness and flavor delivery, the ice cream made possible by Reuben's attention to detail created a whole new eating experience.

Back in 1975, Kevin suggested that Doris open her own dipping store and coached her through the planning process. It was about location, location, location. She was set on a mid-Manhattan spot—in the heart of chic shopping at the corner of 59th Street and Third Avenue, right near Bloomingdale's, one of New York's trendiest department stores.

When Doris broached the subject to her father, Reuben said he felt an aggressive effort to franchise dip stores would be "diluting our strength." For the first time, Reuben said he wanted to sink $100,000 into advertising, that it was time to try it. Doris said she would take $30,000 and get him all the publicity he needed, and Kevin pushed her cause and promised to work with her. Reuben gave in and let her have what she wanted.

Doris tried to coax Bloomingdale's into leasing her space, but they weren't receptive. So she made an appointment to see Robin Farkas, one of the owners of Alexander's—right across the street from Bloomie's—and made a presentation. Though he was more receptive, a deal could not be ironed out. Doris went on to choose a site in Forest Hills, Queens, one of the trendiest areas and one of the highest-volume shopping districts in New York City. But the space proved untenable for a dip shop and eventually this location fell through as well.

Then Doris found a space on Montague Street in Brooklyn Heights, just across the East River from Manhattan at the foot of the Brooklyn Bridge. The Heights is the Greenwich Village of Brooklyn, and Montague Street is its Bleecker Street; the Promenade, the walkway with a view of the Manhattan skyline, its Washington Square. The local supermarkets sold a considerable amount of Häagen-Dazs and Baskin & Robbins had a dip store right

Rose, Reuben, Doris and Kevin.

across the street. Doris found a local dentist operating out of a storefront in the middle of the block and persuaded him to move to the back of the building and allow her to rent the front.

The store opened early in the afternoon of November 15, 1976. The paint was still wet when the first customer came in. Doris realized she had no change in the cash register and hustled down to the subway station, where she was able to get some. They soon ran out of napkins and borrowed a few from the Baskin & Robbins.

The fresh, light look of the place and the celebrity ice cream were an irresistible combination. The "Scandinavian" look reflected the brand's marketing allure and its "imported" aura. The wood trim was light blond; the red logotype was on white background, in a neat, uncluttered space. It was no-frills, it was sophisticated, and it was the '70s—with a repeat logo on both store and packaging. In time, there were sleeves for the ice cream cones and all-natural toppings from Alpha Aromatics, the company that made the Häagen-Dazs toppings.

Doris literally lived in the store day and night. Within a month she began attracting customers. Soon the lines started to grow; there was a buzz that got louder and louder, and by the spring of 1976, the store became a big success. It was like reliving my tie sale in the Bronx—people couldn't resist joining a crowd.

"When people ask me where I was born, I tell them in an ice cream freezer," Doris once told a reporter. "For a year, I all but lived at the store, often sleeping there all night," Doris said.

Afterwards, she began opening more "dipping" stores around the country. After opening 20 of them, we formally established Häagen-Dazs Franchise, Inc. By 1979 there were 30 franchise operations, and the number kept growing.

ℭHAPTER Nine

—No pain, no gain.

In the meantime, Häagen-Dazs' national image kept growing. Larry Muney was in New York asking people to become distributors, but the Glickman setup was about to collapse, and that presented a real problem. Glickman was the New York foodie distributing Häagen-Dazs in Los Angeles. His subsequent deal with Arden Farms, a major player in the California dairy industry, gave them the right to manufacture and distribute our product in the west.

Arden was a huge operation and classed Häagen-Dazs as a pricey novelty item that never took off in a "big way." Reuben would get excited over the sale of 50 gallons of ice cream, but Arden didn't. For them, Häagen-Dazs was a very minor part of their business. Eventually, they told Reuben they would no longer manufacture his ice cream and might even end distribution because we had no real presence in Los Angeles.

Ultimately, it was a bad decision to put a little product like ours into a big company like Arden and expect it to work. Reuben felt besieged. He faced losing odds and the prospect of more wasted money. But he believed, heart and soul, that Häagen-Dazs was a winner and something had to be done.

Reuben and Kevin met with Arden, who gave us 90 days to develop alternative production and distribution capabilities—and then was going to pull the plug on our relationship. Arden did agree, however, to continue to deliver our ice cream to the accounts they already had, although there weren't many.

Reuben and Kevin had dinner in Hollywood and tried to plan their next moves. It was a crying shame to throw in the towel. Häagen-Dazs was a great product and California was the ideal place to be selling it, 12 months of summer a year they thought. But what they learned from watching one store quickly put an end to that thinking.

We had an account in Pacific Palisades that sat right across from the beach where there was plenty of pedestrian traffic. Yet after Labor Day, even in California, the beach people disappeared and Kevin discovered that there was as much of a psychological factor to sunbathing in September as there was to eating ice cream in January. Twelve months of summer, indeed!

"'So, okay!'" Reuben said with the air of finality he used once his mind was made up. "Regardless, we're going to keep it going," and turned to his dinner with renewed gusto. He then told Kevin, "You take responsibility for the thing. See to it the product doesn't die."

Kevin found a small, refrigerated storage facility near the Hollywood Freeway on Santa Monica Boulevard to store the product once it was shipped to California. It was owned by a church, that used it for frozen foods they collected and shipped to a mission in Hawaii. They weren't operating at full capacity and rented out spaces that were so small you could barely fit a pallet of goods through the door. Still, they did have a loading dock, so Kevin leased it for five years. When he got back to New York, we bought two small refrigerated meat trucks to make the runs to California.

Sonny Maldonado drove the trucks to Los Angeles, but we still needed a regular trucker to handle cross-country transportation of ten palettes of frozen ice cream. We found Dave Silva, who hauled ice cream for Dunkirk out of Boston. Silva was also Dari-Farms, a distributor in Tolland, Connecticut, and his son Dennis worked with him. Silva himself hauled the ice cream to Hollywood and brought fresh produce back to New York. He was helpful, flexible and worked with us when others wouldn't touch ice cream because it is such a "delicate" product.

While we established ourselves out there, it happened that Milton Hurwitz's son, Allan, was in Los Angeles as an aspiring actor. He needed to make some money, so Kevin bought a van, fitted it with Styrofoam boxes filled with dry ice, and sent Allan to supply the customers we had and to find new ones. We also needed someone responsible for day-to-day management. Drivers had to be paid, inventory had to be watched and a sales effort needed to be developed. It seemed that every two weeks Kevin would hire someone new for the job.

At about that time, Reuben and I attended an ice cream manufacturers' convention in Las Vegas and ran into Alan Grant, a cousin who'd moved to Vegas and was out of work. Reuben (who liked to hire family connections in this chance-driven way) thought that Grant would be good for our Los Angeles sales effort, and when offered the job, Alan gratefully accepted.

Alan moved to Los Angeles and took over the fledgling operation, and while he wasn't ideal, he was responsible and committed enough to go out and find customers. Most of them were delis that sold liquor. You could talk one-on-one with the owners, offer free ice cream and put a sign in the window without going through chains of command.

Kevin called on the supermarket trade and rode around with the drivers. Their efforts began to pay off as Ralph's and Boy's supermarket chains agreed to carry Häagen-Dazs—the Ralph's on Sunset Boulevard and the Boy's in Marina del Rey had outstanding sales and showed buyers that there was potential.

Though Kevin was invaluable in L.A., he was still our national sales manager, and he needed to get back to New York. Someone would have to replace him in Los Angeles and he thought that Larry Muney would be perfect. Muney was abrasive, but that was just what the situation needed. The next time he met with Reuben, Kevin asked if they could send Larry out west and have him do his thing there.

Muney talked the idea over with his wife Marian, came back, and negotiated a deal with Reuben: He'd go out to California for a year, but Reuben would pay for his accommodations, give him latitude on expenses, and allow him a degree of independence that would enable him to produce results.

Reuben agreed to everything. On Valentine's Day 1976, the Muneys closed up their house in Syosset and went to Los Angeles. Larry executed his patented brand of full court press on our behalf and Kevin was happy as a clam—there'd finally be some steady effort in California and he would not have to travel.

Muney would go out on Sundays and drive around in circles, looking for customers. Week in and week out, he hunted for business in exactly the same way he had back East. He brought in Hughes Markets and the Vendome chain.

"The owner of the building I was living in had about six supermarkets," Muney remembers. "I met him one day and gave him samples. After tasting them he asked me to come up and talk. Actor and television star Danny Thomas was in the building, too. 'Hey, Danny,' I said, 'you don't know me, but I'm going to give you something.'" Later, the actor wrote us a lovely note about the delicious taste of our ice cream.

Larry Muney (seated) with some devotees from
Miami Dolphin country
(quarterback Bob Griese at left).

Muney also increased sales at the "liquor delis," even though we were retailing for $1.25 a pint, which was a lot more than anybody else was charging. We had to be persistent in cracking the market, because in '76, it was still true that almost nobody had heard of us.

Larry gave ice cream to all comers. From February 19, only days after his arrival, through August 10th, 317 stores tried anywhere from a gallon of Häagen-Dazs to a princely eight gallons. He never mentioned how many places told him to get lost. His daily report would list 30 accounts he'd given ice cream to and who would order more the following week. It was the only way to make things happen.

"When you go out there, you've got to chop a lot of wood," an old acquaintance in this business once told me. "And every once in a while you'll get a splinter." Muney's dogged determination to land accounts, his stubborn belief in Häagen-Dazs and the idea that when you start from zero, movement in any direction is forward progress, helped us open the California markets.

As buzz about Häagen-Dazs increased and people tasted it, our sales rose. In addition to the hundreds of liquor delis, Muney took over the Arden network, developing a string of supermarket chains. Sales strengthened, and the reliable combination of Muney's effort and word of mouth caused a groundswell of interest.

A year to the day later, Muney came back East. He had succeeded in establishing a Häagen-Dazs cachet and foothold in the California marketplace. Seymour Deutsch was hired as Larry's West Coast successor in 1978. Deutsch, who had been living in California for years, was a scrappy guy in his 50s with a penchant for sartorial splendor. Reuben found him through contacts in Los Angeles and took a chance. Deutsch clanked along for a couple of years, but because he spent too much time gambling in Las Vegas, the California business never developed to the levels we expected.

In late 1976, Reuben and Kevin began clashing swords over various business issues. Both stubborn and strong-willed, the result was that Kevin left to work for Golden Crest in Connecticut. Except for an accidental meeting in early 1980, when they exchanged a few chilly civilities, the two of them were estranged for nearly four crucial years during Häagen-Dazs's early growth.

After Kevin's departure, Bernard Burkoff became our ad hoc merchandise manager and helped us establish and consolidate the reach of the brand. He came from the Sunshine Biscuit Company in Brooklyn, where he had made his way up the corporate ladder from salesman to sales supervisor, district sales manager, New York City sales manager, and, finally, regional manager, a position he held from 1970 to 1976, managing a 60-person sales force with annual sales in excess of $11 million. In his 25 years with Sunshine, he received numerous awards for his accomplishments, and when he left in 1976, Reuben invited him to come up to the Bronx for a talk.

"Like to take a ride?" he asked when Bernie appeared. Bernie smiled at him. "Sure. Why not?"

They got into Reuben's car and tooled down the Concourse and across the Third Avenue Bridge to a little Italian place somewhere in the Eighties on the Upper East Side. Reuben wasn't much of a gabber, but felt enormously comfortable with his guest, a man not disturbed by silence. When coffee was served, Reuben leaned forward and said, "Here's the way I see it. I've heard a lot about you, Bernie, a lot of good things, and I want you to work for me. Money's not a problem. Whatever you're making, I'll top it. And I'll look after you—you don't have to worry about that. How's that sound?"

Reuben was as good as his word. He left Burkoff to his own devices.

"Reuben came to me," Burkoff relates, "because he needed to get to the next level with Häagen-Dazs. He, Rose and Larry Muney spent more than a decade slowly building up the name through word of mouth and in gourmet shops—a long list of placements in the greater New York metropolitan area. I came on board because, by the early '70s, Reuben wanted a nationwide network.

"The most challenging aspect of the job," Burkoff later recalled, "was getting store managers to give their customers a chance to taste Häagen-Dazs for the first time. Once that was accomplished, they became Häagen-Dazs customers for life."

The network Reuben and Bernie cobbled together was a marvel of oddity. Reuben invariably sought out people who were willing to roll up their sleeves and put in a day's work the way he did. He could smell commitment and dedication as surely as a bear smells honey, and once he found it he was capable of blithely enduring all manner of oddity in his associates.

"His willingness to gamble on untested people was amazing," Burkoff remembers. "We had, as distributors, an ex-prizefighter in Reno, a clothing salesman in Atlanta, a medic in Boise, a housewife and an eye doctor in Seattle, a contractor in San Juan, a restaurateur in Hilton Head, a moviemaker in Minneapolis and a former investment banker in Hawaii—all without a shred of experience. Just imagine a standard-issue U.S. corporation operating like that!

"There's more to the example of that eye doctor in Seattle," Burkoff recalls. "He was no businessman, and in practically no time he'd run up a $50,000 debt. He was really in a hole. Reuben and I went out there and realized just how awful he was. He had a black woman, Yvette Gibson, working for him, who buttonholed us in the hallway of the office and said, 'Mr. Mattus, I can do the job, and I can raise the $50,000 to pay off the debt.'

"When we were alone together, I said to Reuben, 'Honest to God, I just don't know what to do.' He nodded understandingly. 'Well,' he murmured, leaning close, 'if she can do the job, that's all that counts.'

"She went out and got the money, borrowing from friends in Hollywood. She worked so hard and was so

Yvette Gibson, New Jersey distributor
Arnold Strassberg and Rose.

committed, that she even drove the truck while she was pregnant. Over the years she had three husbands, each working for her in the company...and if they didn't perform, out they went.

"Gibson went on to become one of the top Häagen-Dazs distributors in the country, and, as a woman, opened up our government-installation business under new government regulations for minorities and women.

"Reuben had been right about her. In 2002, her distributorship sold for $65 million."

As for the investment banker, the network and system he helped Häagen-Dazs build was based on a group of people who had the same integrity Reuben had, as well as his fierce pride in the product. At one point, Häagen-Dazs was in 15 states, but there was demand in 40.

Keneze Kim, a former investment banker, was another example of the perfect Häagen-Dazs distributor. His wife would only serve Häagen-Dazs ice cream, and when the two met, Kim was taken with Reuben because Reuben, at 65, had the enthusiasm of a 22-year-old. Kim did his due diligence before coming on board to handle distribution in the Hawaiian Islands. Häagen-Dazs was then selling less than three million gallons in a ten-million-gallon Hawaiian market, because what hit the freezers in Hawaii—before Kim took over—was ruined ice cream.

Putting their heads together, Reuben and Kim took six months to figure out how to get the Häagen-Dazs from the East Coast to Maui within two weeks. They even invented a machine to monitor temperatures in the trucks that carried the ice cream across the country and made sure that their cargo containers were plugged into one of the few electrical outlets available on the docks and in the holds of ships that brought the ice cream to Hawaii. Needless to say, the result has been a very successful Häagen-Dazs franchise.

Doris, in the meantime, had divorced her first husband in the '70s. Though she had had three children with Arnold Horowitz, he was an abusive husband who once broke

Reuben in Hawaii.

Doris' wrist during one of their altercations. Though he continued to work for the company, Reuben made it clear to Arnold that if he ever hurt Doris again they would be picking up pieces of him from the floor. Doris met Kevin during one of his many visits to the plant...and love bloomed. She and Kevin, who was recently divorced, married in 1980.

Doris made it her mission to get Kevin to come back to work at Häagen-Dazs. By this time, she was running the dipping store franchise, Natalie was running the merchandise marketing (T-shirts, baseballs caps, aprons, etc.) and Reuben was running the ice cream plant. Kevin agreed to join Doris in the franchise business only and was leery of becoming involved with Reuben.

But a month or two later, Reuben finally called his new son-in-law and former sales manager and told him about his problems in California. He asked Kevin to go out there and investigate and Kevin agreed to go after the New Year.

Kevin flew to San Francisco the first week in January 1981 and drove to Modesto. After making the rounds, he called Reuben from a pay phone and told him he'd soon be heading back. Reuben asked him for a favor: "Meet me in L.A." Although he suspected he was being set up, Kevin met Reuben at LAX and they went to dinner. They talked about this and that, the family and business, until Reuben asked him to meet Seymour Deutsch. The next morning, they visited the refrigerated storeroom in the church basement and spent the day talking to drivers and checking the trucks.

Back at the hotel, Reuben wandered into Kevin's room and asked him what he thought. Kevin thought Reuben had a problem. Deutsch wasn't delivering. Reuben agreed and pitched the L.A. job right at him. "I want you to take over the western states."

Bernie Burkoff was national sales manager during the estrangement years and Kevin knew California could grow into an even bigger market than New York. "What you're

Kevin Hurley.

asking me to do," Kevin finally told Reuben, "is make a big commitment, a big commitment. It'll keep me away from my wife, and I'm not sure she'd appreciate it. There's no way I'm going to willingly get caught between you two. When we get back to New York, I'll hear what she has to say."

Doris told him to do anything he could to help. Marital bliss thus secured, Kevin flew out to California. The church basement, for so long their West Coast storage facility, was falling apart. Conditions were terrible and anything less than optimal can easily ruin ice cream. In three months' time, Kevin found Johnston's Yogurt in Burbank, which had a large freezer on the premises—a 100 feet by 60 feet of good, clean, easy-to-maintain space, large enough to store up to 500 pallets of ice cream. He negotiated a five-year lease.

Larry Muney grew the business out there, and then Doris opened ten franchises. The market began to pick up dramatically. But Kevin wanted to do better. Kevin hired Steve Baker, a hardworking 18-year-old. Steve would do anything you asked of him—go out on a truck, *schlep* things around—and, like Reuben and I, Kevin appreciated people who were willing to do whatever the job required. Kevin decided to groom Steve for Deutsch's job.

One day, Kevin met Deutsch at the Marriot Hotel at LAX and fired him. He temporarily put Baker in charge of the operation, but Steve was still a young kid and Kevin wasn't completely confident in his untested ability. As a result, Kevin hired Golden Crest's Alex Bozzi, a competent salesman with the necessary street smarts to run a business. Bozzi was asked to go to California for 18 months to two years to shore up the operation, and then he would be brought back to work at the parent company in New York.

Bozzi accepted, and though he was officially in charge, he and Baker worked well together. From San Diego to Santa Barbara, we were generating $10 million in gross yearly sales. Bozzi and Baker increased that number significantly, fully justifying Kevin's decision. When Pillsbury acquired Häagen-Dazs in 1984, Bozzi came back to New York, and Baker assumed sole responsibility for running the California effort.

It was a good thing Kevin had Baker and teamed him with Bozzi. Doris, despite her assurances to the contrary, started to complain about his time away, but she had to go along because the business was growing and needed to be cared for. Still, Reuben and Kevin both saw her patience was running out. So Kevin returned to New York—and began the greatest push of all—expanding the franchise.

In 1976, the Bronx factory had begun bursting at the seams. Our word-of-mouth campaign was paying off and we were getting more press coverage than ever. The jolt of energy provided by the dip shops to supermarket sales was enormous and beyond Doris' expectations. We were producing more than a million gallons a year and counting. We put on more help, but the machines could only produce 500 gallons an hour. It wasn't enough.

Reuben—with Milton Hurwitz's help—did what he could to maximize output, but it became increasingly clear that we were going to have to open a second plant, and soon. The two started looking around for a plant that would fit our needs.

Swift Foods, part of the Essmark conglomerate, wanted to get rid of a ten-acre ice cream plant in Woodbridge, in central New Jersey. Swift owned 25 or so ice cream plants and wanted to cut their losses. Salomon Brothers, the brokerage firm in New York City, was hired to handle the deal, and they called Milton, begging us to take Woodbridge off their hands. Reuben was ecstatic.

Reuben told me about Woodbridge. We knew that the big guys wouldn't be interested—they preferred to build from scratch. We were sitting around in the office—Reuben and I, Milton and Tom Mangino, the head engineer—talking about some of the problems we were having in the factory, how we couldn't keep up with the production even when we operated at peak capacity.

We didn't want people to know about the possible move because we worried about how employees would handle the news, how they were going to get to and from work, and other logistical problems. When Reuben and Milton finally took a ride out to New Jersey, they quickly concluded that the plant was too big, but the price was so low we couldn't refuse it. Even with the shabby equipment and trucks, it was a phenomenal opportunity. Reuben and I were pretty sure that we'd be operating at full capacity in a year or two.

The facility stood on a big piece of property surrounded by a chain link fence. It had a guard shack out front, a large employee parking lot, a lunchroom and locker rooms. Compared to our hole-in-the-wall on Southern Boulevard, it was beautiful. The whole interior was tiled, and the floors had a special finish that was easy to clean.

Kevin said that the key to Woodbridge was that it had been a full-service plant from the beginning. Woodbridge was a big, open space with a hardening tunnel. It was also a product-specific plant, built to produce pints of ice cream exclusively. The conveyer was wide enough for 16 pints, which added up to a massive flow of product.

As with all our deals, I was the one who signed on the dotted line. The Woodbridge facility belonged to me, Rose Mattus. With it, I inherited two very pricey Vitaline machines that made pops and other novelties we no longer produced. I sold them to the Joe Lowe Corporation and immediately made back half our investment!

We worked on staffing and executing a smooth shift from the Bronx. We hired a number of Swift employees, including the plant manager, Ken McCarthy, Bill Merritt, their chief engineer, and a number of others. We wanted to renovate Woodbridge as quickly as possible, and simultaneously amass as large an inventory of product as we could manage to tide us over during the transition.

Merritt explained that we had to keep the refrigeration equipment going constantly at Woodbridge because the storage room was insulated with cork and if we allowed the ice to melt, the whole thing would fall down. We had a problem. Because Woodbridge was a union plant, we would need to keep it going 24 hours a day through the renovation if we wanted to prevent the ice from melting off the cork in the empty hardening room or we would have to rebuild it from scratch.

Reuben had already decided to install a Hoyer quick-freeze tunnel—the most advanced ice cream technology in the world. It would revolutionize our production methods and cut down on waste. To install it, Reuben would have to shut down the Woodbridge plant, keep the Bronx plant operating at full capacity, install new blowers and build a new hardening room.

Reuben took Woodbridge off-line for the duration and threw the Bronx plant into high gear. We operated around the clock and kept the pasteurizing machine running constantly to maintain the flow of production. Reuben, Milton and the renovation engineers initially hoped to rebuild the freezer in Woodbridge, install the tunnel and bring in the new freezer by October 1977. But when the three of us met the Hoyer people at a convention in Anaheim, California, in September, they told us that they couldn't deliver the unit on time. Reuben blew his stack and was on the verge of canceling the order. Milton persuaded him that doing so would cut off our nose to spite our face. Reuben relented, and Hoyer delivered the tunnel to us some months later. The pasteurizing tanks, the homogenizers, the cooling plates and all the rest of the equipment were inherited from Swift. It wasn't worth the trouble to move equipment from the Bronx to New Jersey.

Ken McCarthy, the Swift plant manager we hired, brought in Bernie Pajak, who knew freezers and had worked for Swift, and Tom Mangino, the son of our Bronx engineer, who was a bright young engineer in his own right. They supervised reconstruction of the plant and saved us money. Our good friend Aaron Johnson would drive the crew into Jersey in a car Reuben bought for him and served as our benevolent spy—making sure things ran smoothly in the plant. With him on the job, Reuben figured he didn't have to keep a constant watch on things himself.

Three key employees who worked under Hurwitz—Waldo Anderson, Harold Sperodovich and Pajak—neatly illustrated a characteristic of the ice cream world: it's a small one. Milton had employed Anderson as a pasteurizer in the Pickwick plant in Connecticut before they both came to work for us in the Bronx.

After the Woodbridge plant opened, Anderson rented a room in Woodbridge during the workweek and went home to Stanford for the weekend. Milton sold his house in Westwood, New Jersey, and moved to Princeton to be closer to the plant.

Sperodovich, from Swift Ice Cream in Brooklyn, left them to become a freezer operator for us in the Bronx. When Milton left Reuben in 1961 for Pickwick, Stanley Reich was recommended by Simon Levowitz and replaced him. Levowitz also sent Bill Shapiro, another freezer operator, as well as Jack Baker, an engineer. When Milton left, Harold—loyal, hardworking—was promoted to plant manager. He ran things directly under Reuben until Milton returned to us in 1973.

Harold, who lived in Valley Stream, Long Island, was near retirement when we opened Woodbridge and decided he didn't want to make the long commute. His job was eventually given to Bernie Pajak. Shortly thereafter, Milton went off on his vacation. When he got back, he found a note on his desk to call Kevin ASAP.

Kevin said, "You have to fire Bernie because Reuben came in here and started running the show, and Bernie got into trouble with him. Reuben felt he wasn't getting respect from Bernie or his employees."

Milton called Reuben in the Bronx. "What's the matter with you?" You yourself recommended him to me. He's the only guy if something ever happened to me who could take over!"

"Over my dead body he'll take over," said Reuben.

"No, Reuben, over mine," said Milton in exasperation. "That's the whole idea!"

Reuben finally backed off and Pajak became the

Häagen-Dazs troubleshooter—the only one of the original executives who stayed with the company.

The Woodbridge plant opened in the spring of 1978. In our last production year in the Bronx, we made two million gallons of ice cream. We had managed, by hook or crook, to build up inventory and keep our national distribution flowing without a hitch.

By the end of that summer, Bronx production was finished. The old Southern Boulevard plant became a depot. An hour's drive from Woodbridge, a trailer delivered a load of ice cream each day. Woodbridge increased our production and satisfied our customers' demands until we expanded the business even more and built facilities in California.

Closing the South Bronx after nearly 50 years was traumatic. We had produced generations of ice cream in the Bronx plant—from Lea's lemon ices and the Senator and Joe Lowe novelties to the Colony Club and Harmony brands and Ciro's—up to and including the enormous transformations Häagen-Dazs wrought on our lives and the industry.

Reuben and I both felt a strange emptiness when the machines stopped. There was an eerie silence in the building where we had spent more hours than we ever did at home. No one would ever describe us as softies, but we were people of feeling and principle, sentimental in our own fashion, loyal perhaps to a fault, and we both had long memories. The Bronx plant had been a brutal taskmaster, a slave driver that had consumed most of our waking lives, but it had grown over the decades into an old friend, and it wasn't easy to say goodbye to the memories.

Some of those memories involved ideas that looked great on paper but didn't work when we tried to make them happen. Sometimes we ran into unanticipated problems. The equipment we developed in the service of Reuben's ideas—machines that cost thousands and thousands of dollars—eventually wound up filling our warehouse on Southern Boulevard. Visiting that warehouse 40 years later was like visiting a museum or amusement park after the crowds have gone home and the lights are turned off. Sitting there in the gloom was the essence of our ice cream business and the skeletons in Reuben's closet. We had sweated and cried in order to make these machines, and they sat there in the eerie silence, summing up the story of Reuben's inventive mind.

But with the plant in Woodbridge we were now in the big leagues, deriving benefits never before imagined. One day Reuben was wearing a path in our lawyer's rug. Moe Karash remembers this well because Reuben was screaming his head off, accusing Moe of getting him sent "up the river."

"I don't get it," he hollered. "How can I make that much money and not pay taxes? Pay the damn taxes or I'm gonna go to jail. I didn't work so hard to spend my time fighting Uncle Sam and getting put away."

Karash explained that everything was on the up and up. Reuben wasn't going to any prison, but was benefiting from tax breaks offered by the State of New Jersey for bringing business to the area. Having lived all his life never getting anything he hadn't worked for, he was unaccustomed to a government entity actually offering him a break.

By the fall of 1978, Woodbridge had become the Häagen-Dazs exclusive manufacturing facility. With the new equipment and the increased space, production skyrocketed even further. And the big ice cream companies began knocking on the door asking him to sell them the business. But Reuben held out. He wanted to make the world's best ice cream, and he intended to keep it that way, even when he was gone. He told Moe Karash many times that he would not sell to companies interested in producing Lea's cold and sweet stuff. He wanted to maintain the inventory tracking, the ingredient quality and his reputation among the legends of American business.

Rose with the staff at the South Bronx plant.

In addition, by selling the brass fittings in the old Swift plant, Reuben cleared $350,000. In short, he had gotten his new plant for nothing. Between the sale of the Vitaline machines and the brass fittings, he had, in fact, earned a $50,000 profit and had a new factory to call his own.

Only in America.

ℭHAPTER Ten

*—The next generation should be prepared for the
challenge of knowledge.*

As the business progressed more rapidly, Doris was busy trying to turn Häagen-Dazs into a "boutique" item commensurate in presentation with its reputation of supreme quality. She wasn't having an easy time.

Reuben knew that Doris and Kevin took a dim view of Gary Ferguson's East Side dipping stores and other "hippie" establishments that sold Häagen-Dazs. Reuben didn't care what they looked like or what they did, as long as they sold his ice cream. That difference was emblematic of Reuben and Kevin's ongoing, deeply rooted conflicts over positioning the brand. Kevin was a problem solver and impatience was his Achilles heel.

Reuben liked to wait and see, an attitude Kevin called foot-dragging. Reuben engaged in it for years before he decided to open a plant in California. Kevin saw the dipping stores as an exercise in synergy.

Unfortunately, Reuben believed it was his way or the highway, and sardonically would call Kevin "the genius," implying that Kevin hadn't been around long enough to know enough about anything to make a call. Reuben didn't take criticism or advice very well, and neither did Kevin, so it was no wonder they eventually had a huge blowout as Woodbridge was coming on line. Once again Kevin left, leaving Doris to deal with the dipping stores on her own. The Montague Street store was doing very well, and by then she regretted losing the deal with Farkas at Alexander's in Manhattan.

By an odd quirk of fate, one of Alexander's executives lived in Brooklyn Heights, right around the corner from the Häagen-Dazs dipping store. He described the crowds he saw there to Farkas, who remembered his earlier meeting with Doris. Farkas called and agreed to give Doris the square footage she needed. Perhaps because Farkas was so enthusiastic about the prospects of their association, Doris was able to negotiate a 15-year lease with an option to renew. But she needed a fair amount of capital to set up shop.

At that time, the economy was shaky. New York City was teetering on the edge of bankruptcy and interest rates were rising. Asking Reuben for money was out of the question, as he didn't think the dipping stores were worth much.

But Doris was on a mission. Despite the sad condition of the New York City economy, Doris pulled together enough money to complete the 59th Street store—all 321 square feet of it. It opened for business in the spring of 1977. The trendy crowd and impulse buyers soon spread the word, and Doris quickly opened another dip store on West 74th Street and Columbus Avenue, another chic neighborhood undergoing gentrification. There, the landlord was so strapped for cash, he granted concessions just to get the dipping store to move in.

That's when Doris started making some serious money. At the same time, she sensed her father was not thrilled

Doris promoting the Häagen-Dazs
franchise.

with her success and might even be undermining her efforts. They were very close in certain ways, but he was used to getting his own way and found her resistance frustrating. She was the best and the worst thing that'd ever happened to him: strong-willed and difficult to bend. There were equal measures of family dynamics and business dynamics, an often lethal combination. In many family businesses, this formula was both a curse and a blessing. And Doris, like her father, was determined to get her way.

Doris learned about franchising when she attended a dairy convention in Atlantic City and met Earl Swenson, who owned ice cream parlors and had been in and out of bankruptcy. She picked his brain and was consumed by the idea: She absolutely loved her father's premium ice cream and believed others would share her enthusiasm once they sampled it.

The quality image was a huge piece of its greatness, and Doris felt she knew how to market the product to its best advantage and that no one had the passion she did for marketing Häagen-Dazs properly. She was, after all, the brand's heir apparent. Her argument with Reuben was rooted in the definition of the Häagen-Dazs image. She felt that Reuben didn't understand that people were debasing the brand appeal by selling it in the wrong environment and without style.

In the summer of 1977, she and Reuben had a major blowout when he went over her head and sold a franchise to people she felt couldn't handle the product properly. "Oh, do what you want," he finally muttered with a dismissive wave. "I'll send them all to you, and you do what the hell you want with them!" That was the next to last time he got in her way when it came to developing the franchise.

Once Doris got the green light, she wasted little time building her network. Twenty shops had opened before she formed her licensing company, but she convinced all the old franchisees to join her organization without paying the franchise fee.

Reuben doubted that Doris's clutch of ice cream parlors would ever amount to much—until she showed him the money. At the time, Doris owned only two of the stores— the one in Brooklyn and the one on East 59th Street in Manhattan. She was working her tail off for the same $15,000 a year her father given her to lure her away from McCormack. He never even thought of giving her a raise because he figured she had money coming in.

In fact, he still wasn't convinced her efforts were good business. But when he saw the bottom line in 1977 his eyes popped: The two stores alone were bringing Reuben $50,000 to $60,000 a week in wholesale trade.

Doris correctly predicted that if a dip shop were opened in a neighborhood, supermarket and deli sales in the neighborhood would go up. They did. It took a while, but eventually Reuben called the franchise "my daughter's stores." Sales rose because Doris was developing the product's cachet as hip, happening, and so hot it was cool.

The Häagen-Dazs Dessert Shoppe in Fort Lee, New Jersey, was a good example of how that combination worked. Opened in 1977, the place was run by Bill Bromley, an attorney from Hackensack and Steve Eller from Rockland County. They opened with no advertising and were packed every night. "The big attraction," wrote a *New York Times* food critic, "is the ice cream, helped enormously by the surroundings; these include butcher-block tables and bleached wood and leather chairs . . .[for] people [who] like to linger over coffee and dessert after a good dinner, the entrepreneurs employ a classical and a flamenco guitarist to play. From time to time, they are joined by folk singers."

One day Reuben, who decided to talk to Doris again, told her he'd hired someone to build the franchise company. "I want you to meet him," he said. "And I want you to be open-minded about it."

Doris was livid.

Carl Paley, a sturdy man of medium height, was in his early 40s and was the franchising director for Carvel Ice Cream. He was also a rabbi, and very bright.

"Well," she asked him, "what do you know about franchising?"

He described the way he managed the very successful Carvel operation.

"Yes," she said, "but we're not at that point yet. Do you know how to get a store built?"

"No," he confessed, "but I sure do know how to sell franchises."

She left him with the impression that she would do anything in her power to see that he didn't succeed unless she knew exactly what he was doing. Doris was persuaded that her father's plan was nothing more than his way of controlling her and there was no way she would take it.

Paley spent six months trying, but he failed to establish a single Häagen-Dazs franchise. He finally came to Doris and said, "Okay, I give up."

She put him to work setting up a separate corporation for the franchise. It had to be completely autonomous. They had to be able to hire their own people and they would set up an office in White Plains, New York.

Doris got everything she wanted except the office in White Plains. Reuben forced her to open an office at 560 Sylvan Avenue in Englewood Cliffs, New Jersey, where she'd be closer to our house in Woodcliff Lake. He gave her three small rooms: one for her, one for Paley and one for their secretary.

From the beginning, the division of responsibility was clear. Paley interviewed prospective franchisees and helped select those to whom franchises would be sold. He remained their primary contact. Doris met them when they signed the papers. She handled store construction, supervised day-to-day management and the overall operation.

Setting up a franchise had to be in strict compliance with state law. Robert Schroeder, an attorney Paley worked with at Carvel, led them through the jungle of regulations. Schroeder was extremely sharp, though unconventional—he'd often show up for meetings in overalls and a T-shirt—but his contracts never gave Doris trouble.

Once a week, Doris sat down with Paley and the selection committee, which included their real estate man and Kevin, who stayed involved with Doris' business until we opened the plant in Woodbridge. The committee's responsibility was to decide which applicants to approve and to choose locations.

Doris knew success depended on picking the right people to own and manage the stores. Reuben was fond of saying that "a garden grows best when the gardener's footsteps are all over it," which was one reason he refused to believe Doris' idea would ever work. "How can you manage five stores at once?" he'd ask. "How can you be in so many places?"

The point was that she didn't need to be everywhere at once. Unlike Reuben, she relied on delegating responsibility to people she could count on and, from the beginning, tried to identify them in the pile of applications that streamed into the Englewood Cliffs office.

Initially, her notion of an ideal franchisee was a mom-and-pop shop, where the kids helped out after school and extra help was hired on the weekends. She felt that people who fit that profile would be most likely to care for their investment and would put in extra effort to create the friendly ambiance that would grow the business.

From the beginning Doris resisted handing over multiple ownerships, and said so to Paley. As it turned out, she learned that her initial assumptions were wrong. In fact, the best franchisees possessed a different profile. The most successful owners were seasoned business people who were realistic about their prospects, did their projections and set their goals.

That took some time. The first franchisee Paley recommended to Doris fit the bill on paper, but he weighed 400 pounds. Paley hadn't sufficiently considered the impact on customers of a 400-pound man dipping ice cream, let alone the world's richest ice cream. People would make a connection between eating ice cream and getting fat.

The second franchisee had one arm—Paley didn't realize you need two hands for scooping ice cream. (The one-armed applicant did, however, succeed in becoming a franchisee because he hired others to do the scooping.)

In time, the glitches were ironed out, and Doris realized her dream. Like her father, she had a powerful presence, high standards, a clear vision of where she wanted to go and the capacity to adapt to changing conditions. Unlike him, she also had an instinctive ability to supervise by remote control, something Reuben, with all his great gifts, never managed to acquire.

In 1978, when Doris's trademark dip stores were opening at a pretty rapid clip, she confronted her father once again, this time about the way the profits were being split up. "It's ridiculous," she said to him. "You're still paying me $15,000 a year, and I'm bringing in a fortune for you. I want an ownership stake."

Reuben glared back. "What are you talking about? You're making plenty of money—you have five stores of your own."

"Now, you listen to me," she warned. "I didn't start this franchise to be left out in the cold."

"Doris, I can't give you the whole company," he retorted. There followed another one of those dead silences I dreaded, the kind where you could hear the air conditioner whining in the background.

"All right," he caved in. "I'll give you a piece of the main company. In exchange, you take a third of the franchise company, and your mother will take a third, and I'll take a third. How's that?"

"Okay," she said. "Okay."

Doris continued to receive her $15,000-a-year salary until 1981, when she was given a raise to $35,000 plus performance bonuses. Her father may never really have grasped the franchising concept in a legal sense; on the other hand, he didn't exaggerate Doris's financial position. She was making hundreds of thousands a year from her own stores and before everything was sold to Pillsbury, owned a stake in nearly 200 stores across America and around the world.

By 1982, the number of stores rose to 250, and, a year later, there were 369 Häagen-Dazs dip stores in the United States, with outlets as far east as Hong Kong and Singapore. The stores represented 12% of the business at that point, about $10 million worth of ice cream purchased each year from Reuben. Gross sales easily tripled that amount.

Häagen-Dazs's quality and consistency, always very high because Reuben was such a fanatic on the subject, improved even more. The Hoyer tunnels froze a pint solid in a single hour and bulk containers in four. It meant that merchandise entering storage no longer needed hardening. In the Bronx, the temperature of the hardening room went up when freshly made ice cream went into it—and if it wasn't perfectly adjusted the ice cream would crystallize, causing deterioration in taste and mouth feel. Since the new ice cream going into storage in Woodbridge was already frozen to perfection, we were able to avoid any problems. It also became possible to make a load of ice cream in the morning and ship it out the same afternoon, giving us enormous flexibility in responding to market needs.

As we increased the capacity of the Woodbridge plant over the years, we completely revamped the pasteurizing equipment. We computerized everything. You could punch the formula into the computer, hit a button and it would pump the required amount of ingredients through automatic valves, reducing the chance of human error. It also took less manpower.

We employed over 200 people in Woodbridge, including all the old-timers. We had a good relationship with the union, too. Since Reuben was never one to deal with confrontational issues, the union was always my venue. I was the one who had to deal with the delegates.

Years earlier I had made my peace with the union, after having a run-in with a thieving shop steward. At the

Bronx plant I had caught him with his hands in the till. I called the union delegate and told him the man had to go. But because the issue involved the shop steward, the delegate gave me a song and dance that I couldn't fire the guy. I finally got into his face and told him, "You're pushing me up against a wall. Either that guy goes or you'll tell your people that I'm putting a lock on the door and closing the place down. You're not going to force me to keep this guy." Of course he went, and since then I'd had a positive relationship with the union people. We'd even go to conventions together.

Once in Las Vegas I gave them all a good laugh. Tired after dancing for a long time, I sat down in what seemed a likely seat. The delegate soon came over to me and said, 'Rose, you have to get up from here.' 'Why?' I asked. 'Because this is where the hookers sit,' he said, pulling me away. I still chuckle remembering that one!

In the new plant we would run about ten flavors of Häagen-Dazs in pints and bulk containers, and we reintroduced ice cream pops and other novelties as Häagen-Dazs innovations. Vanilla, chocolate and strawberry accounted for 90% of the business—not just ours, but everybody else's—and they still do.

Milton recalls having a big argument with Reuben when he insisted on expanding refrigeration capacity in Woodbridge. Reuben thought he wasn't using storage efficiently enough, and Milton finally lost it at a meeting in 1981. He told him he was prepared to resign [again] if he didn't get what he wanted. We were running about five million gallons out of the plant then, maybe even more. Milton knew there'd be no way to hit bigger numbers one day without that extra storage, and if he didn't get it now, Reuben would blame him later.

By then, the freezer was turning over—completely emptying itself of the product—three times a week. Reuben was, I must admit, very difficult to convince. "Wait and see" was Reuben's modus operandi until he was ready to move on something. His philosophy of life, Kevin would say, was, "If you don't know what to do, do nothing."

Reuben and I had offices in Woodbridge, but we rarely used them. Though we paid regular visits to the new plant, we retained our base in the Bronx. Reuben had perfected the product so that changes to the formula were neither required nor contemplated. Now he wanted to be involved in merchandising and sales instead, where he felt he could do some good. Reuben also felt more at home in the Bronx, an environment of familiar scale that allowed him to keep a close eye on the distribution operation. He was happiest talking to his drivers when they came back at the end of the day.

I stayed with him at Southern Boulevard, but I went to Woodbridge more often than Reuben did—a couple of times a week. I hired a new comptroller—a taciturn, even-tempered and conservative thinker named Gordon Mills—and a payroll officer. I kept my finger on the financial pulse of the Woodbridge plant, got statements once a month to see how the business was going, paid the bills, and issued the payroll. For Reuben, the Woodbridge facility was too big and he never felt completely at home in it.

Reuben asked Kevin to set up his own office in Woodbridge in 1980. Over the next few years, Kevin remembers asking Reuben to come down and rub shoulders with old and new employees. People loved to say they worked for Häagen-Dazs Ice Cream because it was such a celebrity product. Visits from the boss boosted morale, especially in people who'd never worked on Southern Boulevard or never had a chance to meet Reuben before.

Reuben was reasonable about leaving Milton to himself in Woodbridge. But if Milton wanted to spend real money on something—like the expanded storage space—he had to argue for it, which ultimately meant arguing with me. Reuben, God bless him, never changed when it came to money. He'd always been cautious, but he was also a dreamer capable of chasing expensive rainbows. Compared to that, saving money ran a poor second.

Hard at work in the South Bronx

Aside from the big-ticket items, Milton didn't need a budget. Reuben relied on and trusted him implicitly, because he knew Milton watched his production costs very carefully, knowing to the penny how much any ingredient cost us. Whenever our profit margins started to shrink, the man would tell us it was time to raise prices.

In the early days, I once caught the egg man cheating Lea on the weight of canned eggs by weighing the cans. It could get crazy trying to keep track of what was coming in. When a load of fresh cream arrived in a tank truck, we could have used a meter to check on the amount of cream being delivered. But that wasn't enough for Reuben. With such dramatic increases in the quantities of raw materials reaching us daily, he wanted real accuracy introduced into the measurement system, so we put in our own weigh station. Every tank was checked when it came in and when it left. If it showed up weighing 50,000 pounds and left weighing 40,000, we knew for certain we'd received exactly 10,000 pounds of cream (or any other product being shipped to us).

We also put automatic weight-checking machines on the production line to record the weight of every single package we made. As a safety measure, we installed a metal detector to ensure that no foreign matter would leave the plant in a container of Häagen-Dazs—just in case a piece of the machinery would break off, or a bit of metal from somebody else's machine would find its way into the mix from fruit or nut boxes.

The demand for Häagen-Dazs meant getting product out there. Kevin hired Jim Watson from Beatrice Foods to route our distribution. Soon we were sending out six or seven truckloads—50 to 60 thousand gallons of ice cream—a day.

Then, in 1982, we went to the food show in Paris, where Hoyer presented its equipment using Häagen-Dazs Ice Cream as its focus. Hoyer took Milton to Nantes, where the company showed him its best ice cream plant. Milton was so impressed that Hoyer then flew him to Aarhus, in

Denmark, where there was more equipment in place. As a result of his trip we bought our first Hoyer freezers.

That's when Reuben and I were on top of the world, thriving as we never had before. Reuben had finally achieved the recognition that had eluded him for decades. Famous people suddenly became "friends." Honors, testimonial dinners, and requests for philanthropic donations began to come our way. Long gone was the rakish moustache Reuben sported in his youth and the handlebar mustache and Van Dyke he wore in the '60s. During the period of our greatest expansion, Reuben grew a full gray mustache and beard—sober and realistic, befitting a man then entering his seventh decade. It all looked great. But the truth was different; we were getting pretty tired and we weren't getting any younger.

"The Gold Plate" of the American Academy of
Achievement awarded to Reuben, June 26, 1982,
New Orleans.

Reuben, Rebbitzen Esther Jungreis and Rose with
New York City Mayor Rudy Giuliani.

The Mattuses and the Powells.

&HAPTER Eleven

—Age is a question of mind over matter. If you don't mind, it does not matter.

In 1982, more than 15 years after we began making hippies with the munchies happy with Häagen-Dazs Ice Cream, Reuben and I came to a crossroads in our lives. Reuben was smoking four packs of cigarettes a day and it was finally catching up with him—his health began to suffer. Although he quit cold turkey, he did need surgery, and during a long recuperation he decided it was time to sell his greatest achievement, the company that had made him the Emperor of Ice Cream.

Over the years, the double-digit yearly growth of the business had created tremendous strains, internal friction and lawsuits from distributors that profoundly distressed him. All his life he had been an innovator, a man of great ideas, but the sludge and dross of the modern business world was taking its toll and he was just no longer relishing the day-to-day challenges of his empire.

Reuben and Rose with Doris, Kevin
and the grandchildren
promoting Häagen-Dazs.

So one fateful day he called for a meeting with Kevin at the Red Oaks Diner in Englewood Cliffs, New Jersey, and said he needed help convincing our daughter that it was time for a sea change in our lives—it was time to sell out. Doris had been the founder of the Häagen-Dazs franchising company, that part of Häagen-Dazs that supplied some 350 retail outlets. Reuben knew he couldn't sell his business without selling hers.

Wary of getting caught in a war between his wife and his father-in-law, Kevin tried to be as impartial as he could. Reuben had the right to cash out. He had worked very hard for a little peace and quiet and now had a right to it. Doris, however, resisted, torn between her personal goals and accepting her parents' right to reap the benefits of their work. Though she didn't want to sell, Kevin showed her that the two companies were so intertwined, that her dip shops—the Häagen-Dazs stores—didn't really have independent support. When she offered to buy her father out, Reuben adamantly refused because he didn't want her to be a slave to the business, as he and I had been. Finally she acknowledged that her father was right. But Doris, who had been so dedicated to the founding and management of the dipping stores, insisted on a sale to a company with a good fit, one that would grow the franchise and support it.

As a result of that meeting, Kevin, Doris and Reuben met with Lipton President Blain Hess and Vice President Jim Richards. At the time, Lipton owned a perennial ice cream favorite, Good Humor Ice Cream, and had expressed interest in Häagen-Dazs. Unilever, at the time Lipton's parent company, was probably the largest marketer of ice cream in the world.

While Doris was not thrilled with selling her business, it soon became clear that Unilever wasn't planning to keep it going. They had no interest in the dipping stores, no experience, in fact, with any kind of retail. When Doris asked how Unilever would deal with the Häagen-Dazs franchise operation, Hess indicated they would probably close it down. That ended any further negotiations.

Reuben, who was tired and eager to get out, was unenthusiastic about looking for someone to buy his company, but he didn't have to wait very long. During the Reagan years, the rage for mergers and acquisitions exploded and Häagen-Dazs was on every major food company's acquisition list. General Mills contacted him, as did Labatt's in Canada—the Baskin and Robbins licensees there. In order to save time and energy, Kevin and Doris screened the applicants. Then Mike Platt at Pillsbury asked if they wanted to sell.

Pillsbury was a good fit for Häagen-Dazs since it owned a number of successful franchises: Burger King, Steak & Ale and Bennigan's. Platt seemed particularly fascinated with the dipping shops. Although they constituted only 12% of the business, Platt and other people at Pillsbury understood their potential. They were looking to buy Häagen-Dazs, the big business, but what they were really interested in was the 350-shop franchise.

Pillsbury and Doris talked about opening hundreds of such stores. There was an enormous amount of money to be made, and as long as the current franchisees made out well under the new system, the parent company would, too.

Pillsbury had the expertise and an established system for support, and the growth potential they offered for the franchise made Doris especially receptive. Senior Pillsbury executive Charles McGill subsequently made arrangements to talk to the Mattuses, thereby kicking up the seriousness of the negotiations by a notch or two.

Pillsbury was an American icon exactly 100 years older than Häagen-Dazs, and certain features of their histories were similar. In 1869, just after the close of the Civil War, Charles Pillsbury of New Hampshire, a man with Reuben's entrepreneurial daring, arrived in Minneapolis, a city of 18,000. Without the slightest experience in flour milling, he and his relatives bought one-third interest in the Minneapolis Flour Mill, a dilapidated operation on the Mississippi River. Pillsbury met with the local farmers in his little wooden shack and managed to show a profit the first year. About twenty years later, Pillsbury's "A" mill, the world's largest, set a one-day production record of 5,107 barrels of flour. Five years later, the company owned the largest flour mill in the world.

In 1900, Pillsbury held its first recipe contest, offering cash prizes of $680. By 1929, Pillsbury cooking shows were on national radio. In the late 1930s and the 1940s, Pillsbury produced convenience foods—cake, pancake, piecrust and hot roll mixes. In 1949 Pillsbury's established the Pillsbury Bake Off, soon becoming an American institution. By the early '70s Pillsbury focused entirely on food. Over the next decade, acquisitions accounted for almost half its growth. The call for Häagen-Dazs came in January 1982; due diligence began.

It didn't take very long to close the deal, and the whole thing was settled on a handshake. As part of the deal, Woodbridge Sweets was created as the Häagen-Dazs production company in New Jersey.

Right from the beginning Pillsbury asked for very little, but insisted on controlling the accounting. It put its people into Häagen-Dazs and Häagen-Dazs Shops to quickly get a handle on the companies' data. Reuben became chairman of Häagen-Dazs and Kevin its president. Doris was President/Shops, and Milton became Vice President of Manufacturing. Evan Salmore, Häagen-Dazs' lawyer, was put on retainer. Reuben reported to Bill Spoor in marketing; Kevin reported to Jack Stafford, president of the Consumer Foods Group, responsible for supermarket products— refrigerated, dry, and frozen. Doris reported to Norman Brinker—an industry heavyweight. I was given a one-year contract to assist with accounts payable and receivable.

Since Pillsbury was a publicly owned company, federal regulations governed the manner in which its financials had to be reported. McGill had wanted to do an all-stock deal—Pillsbury was trading at $46 a share on the New York Stock Exchange—but the family decided it would take cash instead. I told Kevin I wouldn't be able to sleep nights with people in Minneapolis looking after my money.

(Kevin still reminds me that Pillsbury's stock over the next five years went to $85 and split, went back up to $85 and split again, and was bought by Grand Metro at $88 a share.) They also decided to officially close the deal when the "honeymoon" would be over (in July of '82) since Reuben wanted to test the resiliency of their relationship with Pillsbury.

As a result, during their six-month "honeymoon" period, Pillsbury sent people to the accounting offices three times a week to do due diligence and filed with the government to make sure the deal was not in restraint of trade. While everyone waited, Pillsbury wooed us and the Hurleys with dinners, theaters and limos. Nothing would scotch the deal.

After the sale, *The New York Times* covered the story, describing Häagen-Dazs as a "family-owned ice cream chain with an elite image." One Wall Streeter said, "The Häagen-Dazs acquisition seems to be one of the more tantalizingly interesting ones."

Despite the large sum of money that Reuben and I were to receive, Reuben never seemed fazed by the posh offerings Pillsbury was making or our prospective wealth.

Donald Miller, our accountant, recalled after the sale: "On a number of occasions after work, Reuben and Rose would go out for supper and include me as well. The usual spot was a small kosher delicatessen in the Bronx. The normal meal would be a corned beef and pastrami sandwich, shared French fries and two Dr. Brown Cel-Rays. I frequently ordered a hot tongue and tomato sandwich with Dr. Brown Cream Soda.

"When the business was sold, the entire family stood outside near where the final paperwork had been signed. There were discussions as to where to have dinner to celebrate the sale of the business. All the top restaurants in New York City were mentioned as possibilities. Reuben looked at me and said, 'Where would you like to have dinner?'

"I looked at Reuben and asked myself why he would ask me that question? I then realized that he wasn't interested in what I wanted, but used me as a way of getting what he really wanted, which was a simple deli meal. My response was right on target. "I want my hot tongue and tomato sandwich," said I.

"Reuben grinned from ear to ear. Rose was ready to question my sanity, but quickly changed her mind when she saw Reuben's happy face. No one else in the group was aware of what had happened and they continued to try to convince me that my choice was inappropriate for the occasion. All this discussion continued with various elegant choices bandied about, but to no avail. Both Reuben and I won out! Deli it would be, and we all adjourned to the Second Avenue Deli, a well-known spot in New York. Reuben at that point could have anything and go anywhere he wanted, but he sought to return to those times and places in which he found great comfort."

Don was so right. This indeed was my Ruby.

The next day, Reuben talked to the *Times* and said he'd recently suffered from too much success. Like other family enterprises, his "came to a point where the time and effort we had to put in were unbearable."

He concluded the interview with an observation that rings as true now as it did then, and touched me deeply: "For anyone who puts just a little more effort into whatever they do, they will be just a little above the ordinary. We just worked a little harder, that's all. My wife and family are very motivated people.'"

Reuben was very pleased during and immediately after the acquisition. He felt proud and vindicated, and relieved of the burden of running a vast enterprise. We had, he believed, many years ahead of us, and we were going to enjoy them. We would travel, get more involved with the philanthropies we were engaged in for years and generally bask in the glow of well-earned success.

I hoped Reuben could cope with the post-deal blues. I was never as sanguine as he—either about the sale or the changes it wrought. I've seen enough in my life to understand that indeed more tears are shed over answered prayers than those that aren't.

In the end, my obligations were to Reuben, the man who'd changed the whole face of the industry. Häagen-Dazs was Reuben and my whole life was Reuben. He was entitled to do what he wanted with the business. As Ruth said to her mother-in-law in the Bible, "Whither thou goest, there I will go."

ℭHAPTER Twelve

—Friendship is another casualty on the way to power.

The date was July 12, 1982. There I sat watching the handsomest, most hardworking, smartest, most generous and toughest man I ever knew—the love of my life—selling our business. Häagen-Dazs, in which we had invested years of blood, sweat and tears, the business which we had worked together to raise and nourish like a child, was about to change parents. And like a parent about to give away a child for adoption, I was not happy.

From the beginning I had reservations about selling Häagen-Dazs to the Pillsbury Company. It wasn't anything the officials or executives said or did exactly. It wasn't the money. It was a feeling. Call it my woman's intuition, but I knew something was not right.

We lived in Woodcliff Lake, New Jersey, at the time, and we were actively talking to Pillsbury about serious money, but we were still Rose and Reuben Mattus of the Bronx—Rose and Reuben Mattus who peddled their ice cream pops at every New York City parade; Rose and Reuben Mattus who shook *pushkes*, little charity boxes, in people's faces during the Holocaust.

There was something I didn't like about Pillsbury's big corporate office. I didn't like their pressure, their lack of warmth and what I felt was a lack of sincerity. They wanted to wine and dine us, but nobody in that office knew what it was like to be an immigrant, to come to this beautiful country where opportunities abounded and where poor, hardworking people could build a company like Häagen-Dazs.

Pillsbury only knew the end product. Its business school-educated executives neither knew nor cared about what had gone into making Häagen-Dazs our family pride. The ice cream business had started out as a street business and Reuben Mattus, a genius who had grown up in East New York and Brooklyn, was a street kid. He taught himself what it took to market a high-end product to a connoisseur crowd. These executives did not understand what it had taken to make Häagen-Dazs the quintessential luxury product prized by ice cream fanatics the world over. Over the years, as Häagen-Dazs became the premier brand of ice cream, literally the crème de la crème, they could not understand the obsession of the Mattus family with making the best ice cream possible.

While the Pillsbury executives were wooing us, they promised Reuben and I that we would stay with the firm. Reuben was given a five-year contract to act as a quality-control advisor. I was given a similar one-year contract and asked to advise on the financial operation of the company I knew so well. Thirty-six hours after I had—with great reservations—signed on the dotted line, Pillsbury sent a hatchet man from the home office in Minneapolis to fire me. My woman's intuition had been correct.

It isn't often that 50 years of hard work gets translated into actual dollars. But money does not replace the good feeling of being useful in a challenging enterprise. It does not account for the thousands of close working relationships built over time. Those are priceless. Now, suddenly, I was out of a job. I guess some people would be content to receive a huge windfall and never have to work again. But I had worked all my life, and I loved the idea of being useful and earning what I made. Here I was, an active woman in her 60s, and I was being summarily dismissed.

I sent a letter to Jerry Levin, head of the Pillsbury financial office in Minneapolis. I told him that by firing me Pillsbury had demoralized all the loyal Häagen-Dazs employees in the Bronx. If I could be fired, they knew their jobs were also in jeopardy. After so many years of faithful service, years in which we had worked together as family, they were scared.

I sent Levin back Pillsbury's contract and told him to forget about the $150,000 salary I was to be given. "I don't take money unless I've earned it," I told him.

Even today, I smile when I think about what the reaction must have been in those corporate offices in Minneapolis. In their white-bread, Midwest manner, the Pillsbury powers that be quickly suggested that Reuben and I come to Minneapolis, offering to send a corporate jet. I wanted to tell them what they could do with their plane, but Reuben insisted we go.

"Look," he said, "you've got something on your mind. Tell them about it."

We went to Teterboro Airport in New Jersey and, surrounded by corporate luxury, flew to Minneapolis. Reuben was uncharacteristically quiet and I began to suspect something was afoot.

Once we arrived, I was taken to meet the Chief Financial Officer, who was shortly due to retire.

"How many years have you been with Pillsbury?" I asked him.

"Thirty-five years," he replied.

"You're retiring with the respect you deserve from the company," I told him, "and that's why I am sure you understand how I feel."

"Mrs. Mattus," he said, "I really do."

Sitting in a semicircle were all the financial executives of Pillsbury. I noticed Jerry Levin was not there. My seat was at the base of the semicircle, almost as if I were the defendant in a court of law, without a defense attorney at my side. Then the inquisition began.

"Mrs. Mattus, what is your educational background?"

"What college or university did you attend?"

"What was your major?"

"What advanced degrees did you earn?"

I sized these boys up immediately—well-educated, well-groomed, arrogant and wealthy. These were men who had never pounded the pavement in New York looking to make a living. I proceed to tell them that I had received my business education and degrees from the school of hard knocks.

Clearly shocked, one of the men in the group asked me, "How did you accomplish everything you did, build a business like Häagen-Dazs without a formal higher education?"

"The will to do is to do," I told him, "and like my husband always says, 'Nothing is impossible.'"

"But how did you cope with all the problems that arise in business?"

"My husband taught me: There are no problems, only solutions. I believe in common sense, which, by the way, is uncommon, and I love my work. I believe the most important thing is to love what you do."

I took a breath and then decided to ask the inquisitors a question of my own.

"Do you think I am being treated fairly? Money is not what's important to me. Respect is."

The meeting ended, seemingly without resolution. None of these financial executives was invited to a luncheon the top echelon then held for us before our return home.

We were escorted into a formal, wood-paneled banquet hall where a 20-foot table was set for us with the finest china and crystal. A team of waiters served, while Reuben and I were greeted by Bill Spoor, Pillsbury's CEO. They toasted us and drank to our health, but that did not mollify me. I was still without a job.

As Reuben and I were leaving, Bill Spoor escorted me by the arm to the elevator. He took my contract from his vest pocket and handed it back to me.

"Rose," he said, "we are going to take care of this, and you are going to be very happy."

Bill Spoor was as good as his word. Pillsbury opened an office for me in Englewood Cliffs, New Jersey, with a secretary. (Miriam would remain my secretary for 15 years, well after I left Pillsbury. She was a great friend who eventually succumbed to cancer.) The Englewood Cliffs office became a very important location for the company. Many Häagen-Dazs sales meetings were held there.

Even Reuben was happy on the way home from Minneapolis. He had liked the idea of my not working, which is why he did not oppose Pillsbury's initial action against me. But when he saw how miserable I was, he knew I would not be content to just stay home. For me, nothing could take the place of work. And Reuben wanted nothing more than my happiness.

The experience brought home something I had always known: When you know you're right, fight for it. Insist on respect, and you will get it.

And so ended the saga of the Mattuses in the ice cream business. Pardon the expression, but you should live so long....

After we sold the business to Pillsbury, they spent another $25 million to expand the entire Häagen-Dazs setup. They brought in novelty equipment, put in an automated warehouse with everything on palettes and a man to manage the flow in a little heated forklift that had ten gears. But even before the deal was closed, we were already moving to build a Häagen-Dazs plant in California.

For years Kevin had itched to build a plant in California

to satisfy the West Coast. Reuben never allowed it because he didn't believe it was possible to manage by remote control. As an innovator, he could not comprehend a business that wasn't hands-on. Häagen-Dazs was his personal creation, and as long as he retained control of the company, he couldn't be budged. He was unnerved by the possibility that when business outgrew him, he would no longer be able to control his brand and other hands would shape—and perhaps degrade—his greatest achievement.

Kevin explained to Pillsbury that expanding sales had Woodbridge operating beyond capacity. Milton Hurwitz, who, with my support, became Vice President for Operations, knew we were choking on our own success. "But how," Reuben kept asking, "can you control things three thousand miles away? I don't get it!" In the end, whether or not he got it didn't matter.

When the 1982 franchise convention took place at The Pointe Hotel in Phoenix a few months before we joined Pillsbury, Milton outlined the production schedule for the following year. He'd already managed to convince Reuben to look for a plant out west. Milton was told that Pepsi was interested in getting rid of a factory in Fresno. With Reuben's reluctant blessing, Milton flew to Fresno, examined prospective areas, and came back with his report. Milton offered a number of options but stuck with the idea that the plant should be where there were milk production facilities: in Petaluma and Union, near San Francisco; in Tulare in the San Joaquin region, or in Chino, near Los Angeles.

Pillsbury wanted the plant near the marketplace, but Milton was adamant. He told them, "If you are near the cows, that'll guarantee a steady, consistent, supply." He knew that would guarantee consistency in the final product, since the milk would come from herds consuming the same diets. Reuben would be thrilled with a plan that aimed to maintain quality. Pillsbury accepted that priority and sent Jim Pedersen, a vice president with expertise in inventory systems, to work with him.

Coldwell-Banker gave Milton reports on sites in Fresno,

Tulare and Chino. But Pederson let Milton know Pillsbury wouldn't go for Fresno because they had union problems there. That left Chino and Tulare, halfway between San Francisco and Los Ángeles.

The two spent the week interviewing people in both places. In Tulare, Milton met George De Medeiros and was particularly impressed. De Medeiros was president of a dairy co-op consisting of 97 Portuguese American dairy farmers. De Medeiros offered his own space for the proposed plant, because a deal with Breyers had fallen through and left him holding a big bag.

When Milton and Pederson came back to Los Angeles, they decided to look at Tulare more carefully. Land in the area was cheap and unemployment hovered at 18%. The town was willing to grant a number of concessions, including tax abatements. Pederson asked us to wait before we closed the deal and convinced Pillsbury that Tulare was the way to go. Kevin's job was to gather the capital. Pillsbury approved the plan in September 1982.

The plans called for a plant that cost $18 million. Shortsightedly, Pillsbury's board of directors knocked $5 million off because they felt the plant would be too big. Milton tried to convince them that they'd need the larger capacity and that it would cost three times as much to add it later, but they were resolute in their decision. Milton, of course, was right. Exactly three years later it cost them $15 million to expand Tulare.

Reuben was involved in marketing (and had been since the Woodbridge plant first came on line) and didn't participate at all in the design or building of the plant. When Milton had a problem, he called engineering, and they would contact Minnesota to deal with it.

Milton created the most modern ice cream factory in the world and sent a cadre of trained people from Woodbridge to train the new help. Pillsbury wanted to make Tulare beautiful; Milton wanted it to work flawlessly. The plant wasn't unionized, but they made sure their employees were paid a higher hourly rate than the unions were paying. The co-op was unionized and couldn't figure it out. We could afford it because we owned a profitable company.

Money was spent to maintain the Pillsbury image. We bought the latest Hoyer equipment and the latest in refrigeration units. The plant, like the one in Woodbridge, was designed for expansion.

Everything was computerized, but "bugs" in the system held up the opening for a month. We had automatic weight checkers, metal detectors, automatic printing and automatic counting. Very little extra help was ever required, and Milton had carte blanche because Pillsbury had no experience at all with ice cream. Milton built Tulare on time and on budget. In April 1985, just two years after Milton first set foot in Tulare, the plant was running at full capacity.

Once the plant proved operational, the company threw a gala event to officially open the factory. There was lots of print and TV media coverage, and Reuben and I were invited, as were the Pillsbury notables. Reuben was tickled with what he saw and the smiles on his face in photographs of the event were genuine.

Tulare duplicated Woodbridge production and shipped about seven million gallons a year. The overall production eventually reached 20 million gallons. Two years later, we doubled production at Tulare, and brought them up to Woodbridge levels.

By 1987 plant capacity was again doubled, dry storage was added, the size of the production room was doubled, and more freezing units were installed. After that, yearly production in Tulare alone soared to 15 million gallons.

In addition to the plant in Tulare, we wanted to expand our international business, but we tabled those ventures until the Pillsbury acquisition was complete. Evan, Natalie's husband, worked on a deal to distribute Häagen-Dazs in Australia, but it fell through. He was also approached by Mitsukochi, a department store chain in Tokyo, but nothing came of that either.

Tulare dedication ceremonies.

The Tulare facility.

Back in 1981, Suntory had approached us about selling our product in Japan. They were the world's largest liquor distributors and purveyors to fancy restaurants and hamburger joints. They were mainly interested in the franchise division, so Kevin and Doris went to Japan to investigate the possibilities, but that's when the Pillsbury buyout took place and the deal went on hold.

Even before the actual buyout, when the word got out that Häagen-Dazs was thinking of entering the Japanese market, Milton got a call from Hank Wendler, who had worked for Sealtest and Carnation in Japan. Wendler said, "In case you need somebody in Japan, I'd like the job."

Milton thought it was a good idea and told Kevin about it. Then, with Pillsbury running the show, the Suntory deal went ahead. Kevin and Milton talked to Wendler about opening a production plant in Japan. Then Wendler and Milton went to check out the Takanashi milk plant in Yokahama and an ice cream plant in Gun-Ma, two hundred miles northwest of Tokyo. Afterwards, they met with the Suntory people. Hank and Milton agreed the plant was no good and the milk supply was unreliable. The Suntory people were very upset by the news, but soon offered another dairy facility in Hokkaido. The difference was profound. It was just like the facilities in Connecticut. There was a co-op dairy with Holstein cows, about 60 per farmer, all passing their inspection. Milton told Suntory that if they went ahead with some changes we needed in the factory, Pillsbury would approve and Hank would stay on in Japan.

Kevin and Stafford went to Japan to sign the deal, forming Häagen-Dazs Japan. Wendler was moved to Tokyo, and joined the board of the new company, which had a Japanese president. On September 18, 1984, *The New York Times* noted the formation of the "joint venture with Suntory, a Japanese food concern, to produce and sell Häagen-Dazs ice cream in Japan."

The first dipping parlor in Japan opened to immediate and continuing success. Eventually the brand moved into Korea, as well.

Mark Stephens on left, Reuben (center)
with Suntory executives in California.

Two Japanese quality control people soon came to Woodbridge—one from Suntory, and one from Takanashi—to learn Häagen-Dazs standards. We even printed a manual. Though they were at least a generation behind us, they knew their stuff. Suntory was a very efficient company.

Häagen-Dazs also had a presence in Canada; it was made in Toronto by Nielsen's Dairy, a candy and ice cream operation. Kevin made the deal and Milton went up there to set aside some space for the job. The five hundred milliliter packaging was bilingual. Eventually, another company assumed this manufacturing role. Dipping stores were opened, too, and Häagen-Dazs Cream Liqueur appeared in 1985 through a licensing arrangement with Hiram Walker, the makers of Canadian Club in Canada.

Pillsbury expanded its offices to the Glenpointe complex in Teaneck, New Jersey, and brought in a research and development team. It wanted Milton to immediately hire a purchasing agent. Most of his purchases were once-a-year stuff, but they hired a guy anyway. He, naturally, had to hire an assistant, who hired a secretary, and so on and so on.

From there our relationship with the powers that be at Pillsbury went downhill. Kevin left the "new" Häagen-Dazs after two-and-a-half years and was replaced by Mark Stephens, formerly of Sunkist Foods in Atlanta. For Kevin, it was the right time to go. There was nothing particularly notable about it, since he'd been telling his superiors to replace him since early on in the acquisition. He had originally intended to sign up for a two-month stint, but in the end it lasted two years.

Stephens quickly proved the kind of person he was by getting rid of Milton, who still had a year left on his contract. In 1987, when he was 67, Milton had ruptured his Achilles tendon on a tennis court. Stephens saw him being wheeled around the plant with a cast on his foot and decided they had to find a new guy. He told Milton, "I think you could think about getting your replacement

The Hurleys and Mattuses in Canada (1980s).

ready." They found someone named Ron Hein. As soon as Tom Mangino built the plant in France, he quit, too, and went to work for Edy's in Ontario.

When my one-year contract with Pillsbury expired—the one I had unceremoniously sent back to Bill Spoor—I continued to use the office in Englewood Cliffs and make myself available to the company when they needed me. Reuben stayed on as Chairman of Häagen-Dazs.

In the end, it was a bit disappointing for Kevin not to continue because he'd been received more warmly than the rest of us, and treated very well. But Kevin had no real misgivings about leaving. He and Doris were young enough and had enough in the bank to do the things they'd always wanted to do.

On the road promoting Häagen-Dazs.

ℭHAPTER Thirteen

—When you work you have good days and bad days.
But when you don't work,
you don't have any days at all.

Kevin had been in the ice cream business for 25 years by the time he left Pillsbury, hardly a long career to his father-in-law and me. But Häagen-Dazs was as much a roller-coaster ride for him as for the rest of us. Riding that tiger day in and day out was exhausting work, tense, abrasive and unforgiving. The chance to return to a normal lifestyle had grown important to both Doris and himself. Just eating dinner together was something very special.

After the business was sold to Pillsbury, the Hurleys stayed out of the ice cream business for close to five years. They could easily have stayed out for much, much longer. Kevin had no interest in working again, and certainly not in ice cream. They traveled instead, built a home in Long Island and set up a beautiful apartment in Manhattan. They loved the leisure, though it took Kevin at least six months to adjust to the loss of power, the demands, the limos and the ability to move people. It took six months for him to stop thinking he wasn't important anymore just because he no longer had his finger on the button.

Then he and Doris started talking about various business opportunities they might seriously entertain, trying to figure out what they could do that would challenge and interest them, but wouldn't dump them into a rat race.

After the "Me, Me, Me" 1980s, a certain backlash set in—a whiff of austerity and discipline made itself felt in a gradual turn toward health issues. Doris believed in good nutrition and was a devotee of the whole foods, vitamin supplements and exercise programs that more and more of her fellow citizens were beginning to discover. There was a national obsession with low-calorie foods that amounted to near-hysteria. The U.S. Congress, sensing a groundswell of support for these issues, passed the Nutritional and Food Labeling Act. In other words, they were defining standards for identifying products. "Low fat," for example, would mean exactly the same thing for every product, originally "no more than three grams of fat per serving." Doris argued that this nascent interest could be turned into a successful business, and Kevin thought she was making a lot of sense.

First they looked into marketing a low-calorie candy. At one point in the late 1970s, they'd owned a candy store next to the Häagen-Dazs dip shop on 64th Street and First Avenue in Manhattan (they worked in the candy store on Saturday nights), so they knew their way around the product line. Kevin thought there might be an opportunity out there for a low-calorie candy that tasted good because there certainly weren't any on the market.

Tom Block and Tom Grim—the "two Toms," friends of Doris and Kevin—owned a company called Thomas Sweet in Princeton, New Jersey. Tall and stocky, Grim was full-bearded. Block, shorter, round, firm and fully packed, had what Doris calls "a clean-shaven, very sweet face."

Both were hippies in the mold of Ben and Jerry, and they looked like construction workers. Originally from Buffalo, they'd settled in New Hope, Pennsylvania. They were bright, level-headed people and entirely unpretentious.

The four first got together in 1978 in New Hope. At the time, the two Toms owned Country Fair Chocolates, a chocolate shop in town. Doris and Kevin walked into the store one day and got into a conversation. At one point, Kevin mentioned that Doris was a daughter of the Häagen-Dazs family. Block had heard the name for the first time not long before—the brand was just coming into prominence then.

Doris was so fascinated by the shop, she decided to open a chocolate shop next door to the dipping store on First Avenue. They got it up and running and named it Ambrosia. The two Toms made all their chocolates, and soon Doris had them supplying other dipping stores with candy.

The two Toms had a small facility in Whitehouse, New Jersey, about ten miles from Flemington and not far from Pennsylvania. They supplied Ambrosia and franchise locations in Livingston, New Jersey, and Great Neck, New York. A year later, when Häagen-Dazs really exploded, they were overwhelmed and the chocolate thing faded.

Block understood: They'd simply encountered more than they had bargained for. The two Toms' own business was expanding, too. They opened a chocolate shop in 1979 in a space owned by Princeton University. Six months later, the university asked them if they wanted to open an ice cream shop in the space that had opened next door to the chocolate shops.

They knew nothing about making ice cream, but Block came from a food family—his father had run restaurants—so he knew the importance of good quality, good equipment and consistency. Grim, a childhood friend, practically grew up with Block's family, and the two took the gamble, inaugurating Thomas Sweet in 1980. Several other locations in Princeton, New Hope, Philadelphia and New

Brunswick followed, and the two Toms then franchised their operation. ("Doris," Block dryly points out, "still refers to 'franchise' as 'the "f" word.'") They had their successes and failures over the years, but the Toms' core business has stayed very stable ever since, and retains a reputation as one of the best in the Northeast.

The Toms stayed in touch with the Hurleys straight throughout the 1980s. One day, Kevin called from Florida to say that they'd come to realize they could only take so many trips, and wanted to do something again. Doris felt the way to start was to call the two Toms. She talked to them about a sugar-free candy that would be healthy—good for you when you ate it. But the Hurleys had no interest in operating the business. They figured the Toms could do that. They were top-notch business people, and they knew how to hustle.

Block and Grim were interested and did some exploratory experiments at Grim's place. Eventually, they connected with a candy technologist at Knectel Labs, a research and development facility in Chicago, to take them to the next level. They developed a candy with a soft, chewy consistency. The result was a wonderful-tasting form of Ex-Lax. It had enough sorbitol in it to cause diarrhea. But the four of them remained interested in the underlying concept and kept talking about what they could come up with. For a while, nothing did.

One day, in 1991, Doris called the Toms to say that Reuben was interested in doing something, too. But he wanted to do something in the ice cream business and wanted to get together with the Hurleys and the Toms in Atlantic City. We booked an overnight stay at a hotel to make time to have a little fun and talk a little business.

Reuben had been doing what figureheads do in large corporations. His presence at Pillsbury—the advice, the appearances at corporate functions, at the plants and in public relations—ensured the continuity and stability of the product and the legend. In this sense, he was like Colonel Sanders of Kentucky Fried Chicken (whom we'd known well), except that Reuben made out much better financially than the Colonel had. He, too, continued to draw his salary and would have continued to do so, even if he decided to retire. We needed money even less than Doris and Kevin, but like them—perhaps even more—he felt he had to preserve the standards he had struggled so hard to create and to defend the relationships he had with so many loyal employees.

When their five-year contracts terminated in 1988, Pillsbury had the option of paying Reuben, Kevin and Doris not to compete in the business. They didn't exercise that option with the kids, since they knew neither of them would dream of going into competition. Stephens signed Reuben himself to a new three-year consulting agreement, and agreed to continue picking up the tab for the Englewood Cliffs office and the limo driver.

Between 1988 and 1991, though, the winds of change barreled through Minneapolis, and Pillsbury was acquired by the British behemoth Grand Metro. In fairly short order, almost the entire management of Pillsbury and Häagen-Dazs was replaced with Grand Metro executives. By 1991, no one who had been a party to the original acquisition was left at Pillsbury. In October, a few months after Reuben's consulting contract expired, he was called by Ove Sorenson, the new head of Pillsbury, who announced his agreement would not be renewed, thanked him for his services, and followed it up with the requisite "memorial" letter.

If Reuben had been any corporate player, he would have seen it coming, but he wasn't. He was a creator, a seat-of-the-pants businessman who operated differently. His values were based on loyalty and devotion, behavior prized these days, as Shakespeare said, more "in the breach than the observance." Though Reuben understood perfectly well that the new people could do whatever they liked with their business, he felt that Sorenson had given him the brush-off, plain and simple—and it infuriated him. When he told me about it, he marched up and down the hallway, a bad sign I was all too familiar with.

But his emotional reaction may not have been so much to what Sorenson had done to him. Sorenson triggered something much deeper. Suddenly left high and dry, Reuben realized that he had let himself down, that he had removed himself from the business arena too early. The artist, the innovative genius in him, awoke to the obvious: Only Reuben could, or would, decide when his life's work was over. For the next few hours, he just sat in his favorite chair and stared out at the leaves drifting onto the lawn in the sharp, clear air. Then he picked up the phone and called Florida.

When Doris answered, he told her the story and was still boiling mad. "Just like that, just like I was an empty roll of toilet paper."

Reuben wanted to go back to work. I did, too, though I had my reservations about what this might ultimately mean. My husband was 78. In all those years, he hadn't been any more sparing of himself than he had been of anyone else. He'd driven himself and me, and anybody else he could, into a frenzy of long hours and unending effort for half a century. He had a bad heart and prostate cancer. He had also recently developed macular degeneration and was losing his eyesight, though he still managed pretty well in public.

Reuben was the kind of person who needed the proverbial place to hang his hat. Although he remained steadfastly unimpressed by the trappings of success in or out of the office, he still needed to be always engaged in some activity. He wasn't going to change. I didn't have to tell that to my daughter. Though none of us were eager to climb back into the harness, how could we say no to Reuben?

Doris described their recent flirtation with low-calorie candy. Reuben suggested that low-fat ice cream might be a way to go. There wasn't any anywhere in the country— there was only ice milk, which tasted like frozen cardboard. But if a way could be found to make wonderful low-fat ice cream with the mouth feel of the high-fat stuff, that would be a challenge worth pursuing.

Listening to the discussion, I remained standing behind the chair with my hands on Reuben's shoulders. "Okay!" he finally exclaimed. "I like it! Frankly, it doesn't matter what we make, as long as we're back in business!"

The conversation, Kevin felt, was basically a call to arms. Reuben always worked like a horse, but he was a thinker first and foremost, an innovator, a creative type. Other people had always been expected to execute his ideas. And at that point, frankly, we all knew he no longer had the resources to do much on his own.

In Miami, Doris and Kevin talked it over. They certainly never expected to plow into anything as big as Häagen-Dazs again. They both knew it would mean a complete change in the rhythm of their lives. In the end they concluded that they would never have had all the money and leisure they'd been enjoying without Reuben. There was no way they could deny his wishes.

But they didn't want to go back to the rat race either. They decided to present the idea to the two Toms. While Doris and Kevin knew something about candy, Block and Grim now knew lots more about ice cream. And so we met in Atlantic City.

The Two Toms immediately appealed to Reuben. They were, in fact, perfect partners. They shared his work ethic. Reuben, in turn, had quite an impact on Block and Grim. They felt he was a little out of sync with the way business was being done, but he had the best business sense in terms of goals and knowing which direction to take. After all, the ice cream trade was his whole life. He was still a force to be reckoned with, a true leader, even if they felt Doris had her hands full dealing with him. I could have given them chapter and verse.

The new story was settling on the kind of product they were going to make. It wouldn't be just another ice milk. They were going to make a low-fat superpremium ice cream—a low-fat Häagen-Dazs-type product.

At first, we wanted to create a completely fat free product, but Kevin determined that the "crosshair between good taste and product benefit was going to lie in the low-fat area."

We didn't know a thing about making low-fat ice cream. It had not yet been done. We talked to a consultant about the concept and he wasn't very helpful, except that he did tell us about labs at Pennsylvania State University.

Our first batches were mixed at one of the Sweet locations, where Block and Grim would show up with fresh ingredients and Reuben and I would pick up the rest of the tab. But soon the team realized they needed technological help with milk proteins and connected with the university, where they would go every four to eight weeks.

Penn State has a great dairy science department and a pilot plant operation that reasonably replicates a real ice cream plant. Dr. Arun Kolera, the program chairman, was a major presence at the university, and pulled in substantial revenue from businesses willing to risk money on exploring ideas. The income subsidized the graduate program in agriculture.

The two Toms, Doris and Kevin would get up while it was still dark, drive for hours to get to Penn State, arrive late in the afternoon and get down to the plant at six the next morning. They ran batch formulas with calculators, scales and test tubes; they pasteurized and homogenized. Time after time, the effort failed—and cost us a few thousand dollars a day. Finally they figured out what ingredients worked best and refined the formula accordingly.

Unlike fat-free formulas, the low-fat content allowed us to experiment. The more money we spent at Penn State, the better the taste and mouth feel. After a year and a half, they finally developed a good low-fat vanilla base. After each session, Doris and Kevin packed "hot-off-the-press" ice cream in dry ice, loaded it into the car and made the long trek from Penn State to our new house in Cresskill, New Jersey. About an hour before they arrived, they would pull off the road and remove the ice cream so that by the time they got to the house, it would be at the right texture. Reuben wouldn't be willing to wait a moment to taste it, so it had to be just right.

The melodrama would begin when Doris and Kevin pulled into the circular drive in front of our house. Reuben would tell me to get to the door, where Doris and Kevin would stand with their arms full of samples. Reuben waited like a king on a throne while Kevin or Doris, his respectful subjects, came as supplicants before him. I would scoop the ice cream into different dishes and hand Reuben a different spoon for each sample. Then would come the moment of truth. What did the Emperor of Ice Cream think? Doris, Kevin,and I would hold our breaths in anticipation. Reuben would spoon an egg-size dollop into his mouth, close his eyes, roll the cold and sweet treat around on his tongue, just like he used to do at the plant on Southern Boulevard. And just like he would in the Bronx, more often than not, he would say, "No."

With one word, he would vaporize hours of effort and experimentation, not to mention all those hours on the Pennsylvania and New Jersey Turnpikes—and the money that disappeared into thin air. Like Häagen-Dazs, Mattus Low-Fat Ice Cream was a challenge, an exercise in creating overload and enrichment without the punishing calories. We set out to fool the taste buds and to accomplish that we needed to mimic the fat experience and taste without adding more sugar—the Lea Mattus formula of cold and sweet all over again.

After dozens, then almost a hundred samples, Reuben was still saying "no," but Doris and Kevin knew they were on the right track. All they wanted to know was whether or not he thought the low-fat ice cream they were cranking out was excellent. Eighteen long months later, Kevin and Doris felt like they were up against a brick wall.

On one of their last treks from Penn State to Cresskill, as dusk approached—and tired of the 12 hours they'd spent in the car—Doris ordered Kevin to stop the car at a convenience store and picked up a pint of vanilla Häagen-Dazs. Instead of serving the samples directly from the lab, Kevin used some sleight of hand and put two bowls of ice cream in front of Reuben, the ultimate judge. One bowl contained vanilla Häagen-Dazs, the other, vanilla Mattus Lowfat.

Never one to shirk his role, and ever the one for dramatic flair, Reuben ceremoniously stuck his spoon into one bowl, lifted a dollop of the cold and sweet treat to his lips, sniffed and put the ice cream in his mouth, rolling it around his tongue. He was the master at work. He did the same with the second bowl of ice cream. Then he paused and tasted them both again. He was still rolling his tongue around his teeth when Kevin asked, "Which one is the Häagen-Dazs?"

Reuben, the Emperor of Ice Cream, the maven, the man who knew all the secrets of making that quintessential American treat, the man who invented Häagen-Dazs, that man, on that day, picked the wrong bowl. And boy, oh, boy, was he miffed when Doris and Kevin practically wept with glee and danced around the family room.

Reuben went back and tasted both products straight from the packages, and ruefully admitted that the new mix was—well...good enough to bear his name. Once we knew we could make it, we needed to commercialize the product, to figure out how to manufacture it in volume. We needed a plant to meet our conditions, and we found one, in New Jersey. We designed the packaging and created ongoing relationships with a number of firms.

Kevin and Doris and the two Toms took shifts so that nothing at the plant was ever done, night or day, without at least one of them present. They stood and watched as the mix was made and watched it go through the equipment. Then it was tested and fine-tuned until it was right. The whole idea was to create a product as close in flavor to Häagen-Dazs as possible. When we succeeded with the base, we added fresh ingredients with what Reuben liked to call "dairy notes." We wanted something that tasted as if you were eating milk, not stabilizers. We created a product that is lighter than Häagen-Dazs, but not by much. Mattus Lowfat has a good mouth feel, the same kind of indulgent taste as a superpremium brand, without the fat and calories because it isn't pumped full of air.

Original Vanilla Mattus and Original Chocolate Mattus were called that because we used Nielsen-Massey Mexican and Bourbon vanilla mix for the former, and Droste's Dutch process chocolate for the latter—the same ingredients Reuben used for Häagen-Dazs 25 years earlier. We also used Columbian Supremo instant coffee to recreate the coffee Reuben used; we even bought it from the same supplier. What was amazing is that we had gone from generation to generation. One of the Toms or Kevin would talk to the same people Reuben knew from way back when or with the children who had taken over their parents' businesses!

"We all went off to the International Ice Cream Show in Chicago that year," Tom Block recalls. "When we got on the show floor that morning, the response to Mr. Mattus' presence was palpable. He had a lot of trouble seeing by then, but people recognized him and jumped out of their booths for a chance to take pictures with him. It was wonderful. The people were a tough bunch of operators—the ice cream business has always been merciless—but they all knew they owed a measure of their success to him. You could feel it in the air.

"Later that year, when we introduced Mattus Lowfat to the New York supermarkets at the Concord Hotel, I ran into Jerry Greenfield—the Jerry in Ben & Jerry's. When he heard that the Mattuses were at the show, Jerry said he had to meet Reuben, that he was his idol. You don't hear words of praise like that in our world"—from a competitor no less.

Doris, Kevin and the two Toms did everything to establish Mattus Lowfat. Kevin and Doris handled the marketing and the Toms ran production. For the first year or two, Grim and Block were in the office all the time. Once the business stood on its own two feet, they were

Promoting the health benefits of Mattus Ice Cream.

Rose and Rueben tasting the newest
Mattus creation.

able to back away a bit. Tom stayed involved in production; Doris and Kevin, until 1999, lived and breathed it. Kevin sat at his computer for hours playing with numbers, Doris did the packaging and Tom Grim did most of the flavor development.

Doris, who loved a challenge, insisted on capitalizing as much as we could on the Häagen-Dazs connection. Reuben, however, was adamantly opposed to the idea. He felt it amounted to handing the enemy free publicity. He wanted to show the folks at Grand Metro that they made a grave error when they summarily dismissed him, and he didn't want to be beholden to them. Doris thought he was being his usual stubborn self, and they fought it out. By the time I heard the story, Reuben was talking about how great an idea it would be to capitalize on the name. And it was a great idea that worked.

The Mattus name was clearly emblazoned across the front of the container—and the story of the company on the container touted Reuben Mattus, the inventor of this great low-fat ice cream, as the inventor of Häagen-Dazs. At the same time, we legally covered ourselves by also saying that there was no connection between Mattus Lowfat and Häagen-Dazs. That disclaimer appeared thirteen times in the container copy, even more often than "Mattus." We used this same strategy in our public relations efforts, and it worked.

It took four months to get the commercial venture on its way. Initially we had two trucks and drivers, and two people in the office in Fairfield, New Jersey. In 1992, Dennis Hurley, Kevin and Doris's son, came on board, too. He'd been around the ice cream business all his life and did East Coast marketing and sales for Gallo. He was 28 and a graduate from Syracuse University. He'd been working at Gallo Wineries for six years, and was very much like his father—good with people and with good business instincts.

Not long after that, Natalie's children, Michael and Paul Salmore, came into the business, as did Michael Lehrhaupt,

Doris's son-in-law. He and Laura, Doris's youngest daughter, were in Florida and started distributing the product there. Everyone else worked out of the Fairfield, New Jersey, factory.

Reuben was thrilled to have them all come into the business, because it gave him a real reason to build it, to make something of it with his remaining energies.

Mattus Lowfat was very well received. The tremendous amount of talk about health and the importance of low-fat diets helped us build our inroads to the market, and soon people noticed. Of course, not all of that attention was welcome. One of our competitors complained to the New York Department of Agriculture that we were mislabeling our packages because Mattus was not labeled as ice milk. We soon received a notice by telegram that they were going to seize all of our illegally labeled merchandise. Our attorney acquired an injunction and, in the end, the state agreed to stop, after the Food and Drug Administration said there was nothing wrong in what Mattus was doing. But the disgruntled competitor had cost us $50,000 in legal fees.

Soon Häagen-Dazs and Ben and Jerry's were knocking us off. Reuben's magic touch had worked again, and this time his children and grandchildren realized his vision.

In 1993, *Time* magazine named Mattus Lowfat one of the ten best products of the year. Reuben had by then been the recipient of endless awards and commendations, but this one touched his heart in a special way. He felt he had ended his illustrious and innovative career on an upswing, that he had once again become a pioneer of the industry he loved so much, and once again changed the way it conducted its business. Doris and I also won an award from the National Association of Women Business Owners for "outstanding entrepreneurship."

Reuben had traveled a long, long way in the 60 years since taking control of his mother's business on Southern

Rose Vesel Mattus, "Outstanding Entrepreneur."

Boulevard, continuously breaking new ground. From the ice cream itself to the packages it comes in, people were still following his lead.

$\mathcal{C}$HAPTER Fourteen

—Till death do us part.

In the opening days of 1994, Reuben and I took a short vacation to visit friends and family in Florida. For a man who had been restless all his life, he was finally content. We reserved a suite in our favorite, charming hotel in Deerfield Beach. Just before we left New Jersey, he took a physical and the doctors gave him a clean bill of health. His prostate cancer, diagnosed years before, was still in remission; his blood pressure and cholesterol levels were fine and completely under control.

Early on Thursday morning, January 27, we went for a long walk along the ocean. It was a beautiful day in a beautiful place, and we got a kick out of strolling along the boardwalk, breathing in the sweet sea air.

After an hour or so, we returned to the hotel, showered, and prepared to dress for lunch. Fresh from his shower, swathed in bath towel, and as gorgeous to me at 81 as he was as a 17-year-old on Blake Avenue, Reuben sat down on the edge of the bed, pulled me down to his side and told me how much he loved me. This was a new thing—Reuben was never romantic that way. We'd fought about his inability to express his love for me for decades. At one point, I even dragged him to a psychiatrist, hoping to make him see how hard it was to stay tied to him emotionally. "You're a very special woman, Rose," he confessed to me that day in Florida. "I love you so much."

He had never said that to me before. I was his "secret weapon," but he'd never before been what he called "mushy." I smiled and was touched and thrilled in ways only a woman can understand, and was about to tell him so, when he suddenly fell backward on the bed, unconscious.

My hysteria mounted as I called 911. The medical squad arrived in minutes and rushed him to the North Broward Medical Center, but by the time we got there he was brain-dead.

My life ground to a sudden and complete halt. People rushed in to fill the void—my daughters and sons-in-law and grandchildren, good friends—were all caring and loving, but for the longest time I felt entombed in ice. Reuben and I had been married and run a business together for so long. We had seen each other continuously at all hours of the day and night for almost 60 years. We went through so many ups and downs, raised a family together and spent our lives side by side. I lost more than a person or a husband or a partner, I felt I lost part of my own body—and still do—and that's just the way it is.

Funeral services were held on January 30, 1994, in New York City, at the Riverside Chapel on West 76th Street and Amsterdam Avenue. We had brought his body home from Florida. It was bitter, bitter cold, and a blizzard was blowing through the tall buildings of New York. The weather was so bad, the cemetery was storing new arrivals in vaults until the snow stopped and they could dig again. Before one storm ended, another began.

I moved in a fog. Rebbetzin Esther Jungreis, a dear friend and the charismatic spiritual leader of Hineni, a

Jewish outreach organization we supported, made all the arrangements. Reuben may not have been an observant Jew, but, as Esther put it, he had been a righteous Jew and she felt he deserved a righteous Jew's funeral. She persuaded the cemetery to bury him that very day, despite the swirling storms.

People from all walks of life, rich and poor, Jew and gentile, came to pay their respects. There were so many of them they couldn't all squeeze into the biggest of the Riverside chapels, and so they spilled out into the windy, stormy street. Some came from as far away as Israel. The weather was so terrible, I figured no one would show up, but everyone Reuben cared about, who could still stand or walk, was there.

And, of course, there was a small miracle. As we arrived at the cemetery, the sun broke through the gray, threatening skies. Eddie, my brother, now a retired New York attorney, delivered a graveside eulogy. One line in that eulogy stood out: He described Reuben as "my mentor and my tormentor," and then he told a typical Reuben story.

When Eddie was a young boy, Reuben put him to work in the factory in the South Bronx. Eddie was supposed to sweep out the place before he left work for the day. One night, Al, our other brother, and a couple of friends were picking him up and driving to the Catskill Mountains for a week's vacation. In those days, the ride took close to four hours.

Eddie was hurrying out the door when he ran into Reuben, who asked him where he was going. When Eddie explained that his ride to the mountains was waiting for him, Reuben looked at the floor, and shaking his head, said, "That floor isn't swept, and you know it."

Eddie was wild with anxiety and told Reuben he was going to miss his ride, that his brother and friends would leave without him.

"So? Let 'em," Reuben barked in irritation. "You never skimp on your job, hear me?"

But Eddie was a wise guy, slipped out when no one

was looking and jumped into the waiting car. The boys took off, but forty-five minutes later, Al spotted Reuben's car in the rearview mirror, and Reuben was waving for him to pull over. The minute the cars stopped moving, Reuben leapt out in a fury, seized Eddie by the neck and almost pulled him through the window. There were four boys in that car and they knew it was useless to oppose him.

"You were supposed to finish sweeping the floor before you left," he growled at Eddie, "and that's what you're going to do!"

They drove back to the Bronx in a loud silence. Crushed and resentful, my brother finished sweeping the floor. When he was done, he looked as if he had lost his best friend and shuffled to the door.

Reuben, who was pulling on his jacket, caught up with him. "You look like you could use a bite to eat, kid," he said, and dragged him across the street to a luncheonette. As they finished their sandwiches and coffee, Reuben smiled at him and asked, "Where's that you were supposed to be going tonight?"

"Ellenville," the boy replied dejectedly.

"Well," Reuben said, slapping him on the shoulder, "now that you've done your job like you were supposed to, I'll drive you up there. Let's go!" And that's exactly what he did.

To a great extent, Reuben was my mentor and tormentor, as well. He was a man of fierce and unbending principle, a hard but generous taskmaster, a devoted husband who loved me yet never really said so until the hour he died. He was also a great philanthropist, forever helping people and institutions in need, especially where education and the State of Israel were concerned.

On that snowy, miserable Sunday in 1994, I began a long journey back through our many, many years together—a journey I am still making. I learned how much I appreciated who he was and what he accomplished in his time on this earth, and I uncover the touch of him everywhere on my soul.

The New York Times put it this way: "The Polish immigrant who stuck an umlaut on a nonsensical name and parlayed the exotic result into a multimillion-dollar company is gone."

But his legacy lives on.

Rose Mattus, the Empress of Ice Cream.